The Cambridge Introduction to
Jane Austen

Jane Austen is unique among British novelists in maintaining her
popular appeal while receiving more scholarly attention now than ever
before. This innovative introduction by a leading scholar and editor of
her work suggests what students need to know about her life, context
and reception, while proposing a new reading of the novels. Each work is
discussed in detail, and essential information about her literary
influences and her impact on later literature and culture is provided.
While the book considers the key areas of current critical focus, its
analysis remains thoroughly grounded in readings of the texts
themselves. Janet Todd outlines what makes Austen's prose style and
character development so experimental and gives useful starting points
for the study of the major works, with suggestions for further reading.
This book is an essential tool for all students of Austen, as well as for
readers wanting to deepen their appreciation of the novels.

JANET TODD is Herbert J. C. Grierson Professor of English at the
University of Aberdeen.

D0161892

Cambridge Introductions to Literature

This series is designed to introduce students to key topics and authors. Accessible and lively, these introductions will also appeal to readers who want to broaden their understanding of the books and authors they enjoy.

- Ideal for students, teachers, and lecturers
- Concise, yet packed with essential information
- Key suggestions for further reading

Titles in this series:

From *Fragments on the Theory and Practice of Landscape Gardening* by
H. Repton, assisted by his son, J. A. Repton (London: printed by
T. Bensley and Son, for J. Taylor, 1816), opposite p. 58. Reproduced by
permission of the Syndics of Cambridge University Library.

The Cambridge Introduction to
Jane Austen

JANET TODD

CAMBRIDGE UNIVERSITY PRESS
Cambridge, New York, Melbourne, Madrid, Cape Town, Singapore, São Paulo

Cambridge University Press
The Edinburgh Building, Cambridge CB2 2RU, UK

Published in the United States of America by Cambridge University Press, New York

www.cambridge.org
Information on this title: www.cambridge.org/9780521674690

© Janet Todd 2006

First published 2006

Printed in the United Kingdom at the University Press, Cambridge

A catalogue record for this publication is available from the British Library

ISBN-13 978-0-521-85806-9 hardback
ISBN-10 0-521-85806-2 hardback

ISBN-13 978-0-521-67469-0 paperback
ISBN-10 0-521-67469-7 paperback

Contents

Preface

In this introductory study I am offering a detailed reading of the six completed novels of Jane Austen, together with enough background material for a student to locate the works in their historical moment. This is especially important for those novels conceived at Chawton in the last years of the Revolutionary and Napoleonic Wars. I have, however, concentrated on what strikes me as contributing most to Jane Austen's universal popularity: her ability to create the illusion of psychologically believable and self-reflecting characters. Her novels are investigations of selfhood, particularly female, the oscillating relationship of feeling and reason, the interaction of present and memory, and the constant negotiation between desire and society. Charlotte Brontë memorably wrote that Austen avoided the passions, that she rejected 'even a speaking acquaintance with that stormy Sisterhood'.[1] Although in a mode quite different from Brontë, Jane Austen – sometimes ironic, rarely unrestrained – has nonetheless become for me on this latest rereading a writer about passion. I am not suggesting that she unequivocally celebrates it but that, through her representation of character, she reveals a fascination with its literary construction and narcissistic power – and at times its absurdity.

In the eighteenth century, medical writers, experimental scientists, philosophers, and the literate public were intensely interested in the subject of the self, especially the emotional self. Living mammals were cut open to see their hearts pump; less brutally, human beings were subject to almost scientific inspection. There grew up 'an experimental approach to the knowledge of character', so that emotion 'caused by misfortune, evil agents, an author, or a scientist, can invite either objective scrutiny or sympathetic identification'.[2] The novel served this interest through its experiments with character, while its representations often accorded with attitudes in contemporary medicine and philosophy.

In a celebrated passage of *Tristram Shandy* (1759–67), Laurence Sterne's narrator remarks that if there had been a window onto 'the human breast . . . nothing more would have been wanting, in order to have taken a man's character, but to have taken a chair and gone softly, as you would to a dioptrical bee-hive, and looked in, – viewed the soul stark naked . . . But . . . our minds shine not through the body.'[3] Austen's novels allow limited transparency of the feeling body, but only after the reader has done more than draw up a chair.

I have composed the *Introduction* while overseeing the Cambridge Edition of Jane Austen's complete works and a volume of contextual entries. Some of the arguments and material of the editors and contributors have undoubtedly seeped into the book and, following a remark in *Emma*, 'seldom can it happen that something is not a little disguised, or a little mistaken'. I hope I have noted direct influence and I apologise for inadvertent or distorted borrowing. I would especially like to thank Deirdre Le Faye, Richard Cronin, Dorothy McMillan, John Wiltshire, Edward Copeland, and Brian Southam. I have appreciated suggestions from David Hewitt, Derek Hughes, and Jennifer MacCann. In addition, I am most grateful to Linda Bree at Cambridge University Press for her careful reading of the manuscript. My main debt is to Antje Blank for her help and many insights.

Abbreviations

L   *Jane Austen's Letters,* ed. Deirdre Le Faye, third edition (Oxford University Press, 1995), referred to in the text by page numbers.

FR   Deirdre Le Faye, *Jane Austen. A Family Record,* second edition (Cambridge University Press, 2004).

Memoir James Edward Austen-Leigh, *A Memoir of Jane Austen and other Family Recollections,* ed. Kathryn Sutherland (Oxford: World's Classics, 2002).

Quotations from Jane Austen's novels are taken from the *Cambridge Edition of the Works of Jane Austen* and sourced to volume and chapter using the following abbreviations:

E   *Emma*
MP   *Mansfield Park*
NA   *Northanger Abbey*
P   *Persuasion*
P&P   *Pride and Prejudice*
S&S   *Sense and Sensibility*

Subheadings in this book are taken (sometimes slightly adjusted) from Jane Austen's letters, her novels, and well-known biographical and critical works.

Chapter 1

Life and times

Jane Austen is one of the great writers of English literature because no reader and no period exhausts her books. Something always escapes from a reading while every reading enriches. Like the town of Lyme in *Persuasion*, the novels 'must be visited, and visited again'. In this respect the comparison with William Shakespeare, often made in the mid- to late nineteenth century, is apt. She shares with him, too, a rare crossover appeal, achieving both academic and popular status: the object of scholarly analysis and cult enthusiasm. Inevitably there is uneasiness across the boundary: the academy worries about studying work with such mass appeal, such easy intimacy with film and television, while the public has become irritated by the exploiting, deconstructing, abstracting, genderising, politicising, and sexualising of their heroine. Despite differing readerly anxieties, however, nobody can doubt that Jane Austen serves something of the Bible's former function: helping to make a shared community of reference for the literate English-speaker, her work insinuates itself into the way we think and talk – or wish to talk. This is a more visual than literary age, but for many of us Jane Austen's novels still function as the works of Radcliffe, Burney, Cowper, and Scott did for her heroines, saturating our minds and attitudes.

Not a life of event

Her biography depends on written evidence outside her novels, for she is one of the least overtly autobiographical of authors: there is no female writer or witty older spinster in her works and no heroine who rejects marriage as she did or who lies on her sickbed mocking hypochondria. Almost all the information on Jane Austen comes from her family, mostly from letters written to her sister Cassandra, who selected some as family souvenirs and rejected others, long before they reached the public; they begin in 1796 after the earliest works had been drafted. The letters are augmented by pious memoirs from her brother and nephew, the 'Biographical Notice' (1817) by Henry Austen and *A Memoir of Jane Austen* (1870) by James Edward Austen-Leigh, both of which stress the familial, constricted nature of her life and lack of romantic passion. Outside these sources, little is known of Austen compared to her celebrated contemporaries, Lord Byron or Percy Bysshe Shelley for example, whose daily, sometimes hourly, activities and thoughts are documented. As a result, much remains hidden, perhaps her most intimate aspects, and yet, as John Wiltshire has remarked, we have for Jane Austen 'a fantasy of access . . . a dream of possession'.[1] Each generation makes a consistent image of the author, a new commodity in keeping with its own desires: the kindly spinster of the nineteenth century, the baulked romantic heroine of the twentieth, and the ambitious professional author of the present.

Jane Austen was born on 16 December 1775 into a web of family connections, which included on one side the rich and influential Leighs of Stoneleigh Abbey and the Knights of Godmersham and on the other clerics and an apprentice milliner. Her father, George Austen, was a country rector of latitudinarian or liberal views in the village of Steventon in the southern English county of Hampshire, and her mother Cassandra (née Leigh), daughter of a former Fellow of Oxford's All Souls College, had aristocratic links. George Austen had obtained a parish through the interest of Thomas Knight, the rich husband of his second cousin. Later he acquired a second living at neighbouring Deane through his uncle Francis. Thomas Knight owned not only the Steventon living but also the manor of Steventon, with all its dependent houses and holdings. To the Austens he rented a nearby farm, with which George added about a third to his clerical income; together with his reliance on tithes, this must have given the family a keen interest in agriculture and agricultural improvements.[2] To augment his income still further, George took in well-to-do boys to prepare for university; by 1779 there were four pupils living at the rectory. While common for Anglican clergymen, such activity still suggests the rather insecure family status of George Austen, just on the edge of the gentry. It contributed to his daughter's lifelong concern for money and the nuances of class. Although less important than native intelligence and good sense, birth and breeding mattered: being a gentleman or a gentleman's daughter with the manners and mannerly attitudes implied.

George and Cassandra Austen were cultivated people. In his son Henry's words, George, with his library of over 500 books, was 'a profound scholar' with 'most exquisite taste', and Cassandra composed skilful comic verse on local people and events, a common pastime within her community. The pair had eight children. Beyond a handicapped boy who was sent from home to live in a neighbouring community (and is unmentioned in the 'Biographical Notice' and *Memoir*), the Austen sons did reasonably well: James followed his father into the Steventon living; Edward was adopted by the rich Knight relatives, later changed his name to Knight, and inherited Godmersham Park, Chawton Manor, and Steventon, delivering an income somewhere between £10,000 and £15,000 a year; Francis and Charles entered the Royal Naval Academy as young boys, just under twelve years of age, and rose up the ranks during the long Revolutionary and Napoleonic Wars, ending as admirals through their impressive longevity (ninety-one and seventy-three respectively); after a time in the militia Henry became a banker and agent for the army until bankrupted in March 1816 by the post-war economic slump; then he entered the Church. By contrast, the two girls, Jane and her sister Cassandra, the elder by three years, had no professional opportunities and few chances of forming an income. While her father lived, Jane had only £20 a year to spend on herself and give to charity.

In much the same period, the feminist Mary Wollstonecraft was complaining about the restricted lives of women. The only real 'work' that society seemed to sanction was the gaining of a husband and, when genteel, reasonably educated girls remained single, they were regarded as a drain on their families, used primarily to help nurture and nurse their married relatives. Austen accepted the inescapable fact of female dependency on men, and the anger of Wollstonecraft is not openly expressed in the novels, except perhaps by the melodramatic Jane Fairfax in *Emma*, who implicitly compares her lot as potential governess to that of a slave or prostitute, but the predicament haunts all the heroines. At the same time, the duty of care and social usefulness that devolved on so many daughters and sisters is not downplayed or diminished by its unprofessional standing.

At Easter 1783 the Austen girls were sent to Oxford to be tutored by Mrs Ann Cawley, who then took them to Southampton, a stay interrupted in the autumn by an outbreak of typhus from which Jane nearly died. There followed a couple of years of more formal instruction at Abbey House School in Reading, ruled by the eccentric Mrs La Tournelle, known for her cork leg and thespian obsessions. But it seems that the fees taxed the Austen parents and by the end of 1786 the sisters had returned to Steventon, where they were casually instructed within the family by an educated father, mother, and brothers – and more so by themselves. Jane seemed unperturbed by the informality: although she appreciated a well-stocked mind, especially for its conversational results, she had little respect for formal education, even for boys. In her novels fools could not become wise through education in facts; information without aptitude benefited no one, neither heroine nor author. When considering the lightness of *Pride and Prejudice*, she laughingly suggested she might have followed more educated writers by padding it out with 'an Essay on Writing, a critique on Walter Scott, or the history of Buonaparte' (*L*, p. 203). Reading promiscuously, especially in fiction, she felt no need for 'enormous great stupid thick Quarto

Volumes' (*L*, p. 206). Her own slim novels would not be history or comments on history, but the later ones would be aware of their place in history.

Financially dependent on their father, as they came to adulthood the two Austen daughters naturally contemplated a future of marriage as the 'pleasantest preservative from want' (*P&P*, 1:22). Neither sister achieved it: Cassandra became engaged to a clergyman who died in Jamaica from yellow fever, leaving her his fortune of £1,000, and, when she was twenty, Jane briefly flirted with a visitor from Ireland, Tom Lefroy, the nephew of her much-loved neighbour Madam Lefroy, who made sure the young man left before his relationship with a penniless girl became serious. Throughout their lives the sisters' closest relationship would be with each other. A great-niece, who knew only Cassandra, wrote that 'they were wedded to each other by the resemblance of their circumstances, and in truth there was an exclusiveness in their love such as only exists between husband and wife'.

Considering how much the Austens depended on the patronage and interest of their kin, it is not surprising that the network of family members impinged on Jane's life. Outside the immediate family group, one relative especially impressed her: Countess Eliza de Feuillide. Fourteen years older than Jane, Eliza was the daughter of George Austen's sister Philadelphia, who had gone to India to marry Tysoe Saul Hancock in 1753. They had one daughter, Eliza (rumoured to be the result of an affair with Warren Hastings, future Governor of Bengal, a rumour supported by his setting up a £10,000 trust fund for the child).[3] Eliza stayed for long periods in the Steventon parsonage, flirting with the Austen sons and much enjoying the theatricals in which they all indulged.[4] Through Eliza the French Revolution of 1789 impacted personally on the family. Eliza had married a French captain in the dragoons who styled himself the comte de Feuillide; during the Terror in February 1794 he was guillotined while his wife and son were in England. Three years later Eliza married Jane's favourite brother Henry and continued flirting, declaring she had 'an aversion to the word *husband* and never ma[d]e use of it'.[5] The glamorous countess may have influenced Austen's depiction of pretty, vivacious women, from the predatory Lady Susan and Mary Crawford to the sparkling Elizabeth Bennet.

From the age of eleven, probably earlier, Jane had been writing delicious, sometimes surreal stories and parodies to amuse her family – or, in Virginia Woolf's opinion 'everybody' – since 'even at that early age . . . Whatever she writes is finished and turned and set in its relation, not to the parsonage, but to the universe'.[6] The stories are full of anarchic fantasies of female power, licence, illicit behaviour, and general high spirits. Drunkenness, incest, and serial killings routinely occur in speedy kaleidoscopic permutations, revealing even at this early stage Jane Austen's youthful awareness of the comic possibilities of language through absurd conjunctions: Lady Williams's 'handsome Jointure & the remains of a very handsome face' or the advice to beware of the 'unmeaning Luxuries of Bath and of the stinking fish of Southampton' ('Jack and Alice' and 'Love & Freindship'). Each work is self-consciously literary, mocking the idea of realism by exaggerating details of ordinary life, inflating current stylistic habits of hyperbole, and turning common plot devices into parodies of the adult reading to which, in her novel-addicted family, Jane Austen was exposed. These juvenile productions physically mimic the grown-up book: they are written out carefully in notebooks and provided with dedications to Martha Lloyd, 'Madame La Comtesse De Feuillide', and, of course, Cassandra.

At fourteen Jane Austen wrote the longest of these juvenile productions, 'Love & Freindship', a brilliant burlesque of popular sentimental novels. It took two girls through a series of absurd adventures in which, as in sentimental fiction, love and hate are sudden and absolute, female friendship immediate and excessive, familial relationships made and unmade, and emotional extremes paralleled only by the extreme nature of the happenings. While sentimental to the core, crying, fainting, palpitating, falling ill and dying, the central characters are entirely amoral, believing that sensation must triumph over commonsense morality and justify any act of theft or betrayal.

'Love & Freindship' was followed two years later by a work that foreshadowed the mature novels, 'Catharine or The Bower', a rehearsal for 'Susan', which would in time become *Northanger Abbey*. In this story Austen created a principled, unsophisticated heroine of ordinary achievements, devoted to a fantasy life within a garden 'bower' and constrained by a maiden aunt to whom 'all gallantry was odious' and for whom any slight impropriety foretold the destruction of the kingdom. The manuscript ends before a concluding marriage – if that indeed was to be its end. 'Catharine' was succeeded by 'Lady Susan', probably written in 1794 but copied out later in about 1805, a more polished but less prefiguring work.[7] An epistolary *jeu d'esprit*, it was rooted in the eighteenth-century novel in letters, which suited the subject matter of a heroine manoeuvring within a world in which men control property and women make property of men. The female rake Lady Susan, a handsome, selfish widow with 'attractive Powers', enjoys her own energetic duplicity and knows that 'Consideration and Esteem as surely follow command of Language, as Admiration waits on Beauty.' Her schemes fail, but, like the jolly heroines of the burlesque juvenile pieces, she is left unabashed and unreformed, still very much 'herself'.

Throughout her life Jane Austen avoided ostentatious habits and what she called 'novel slang', adhering instead to plain writing and to commonsensical consequences in plots that are none the less tightly constructed. The new 'style of fiction' with which she was credited by Walter Scott in his review of her mature novel *Emma* is implied by the high-spirited burlesques and parodies of these Steventon days.[8]

From about 1795 Jane Austen was sketching out three full-length novels, clearly intended for more than family amusement. One of these, 'First Impressions', an early version of *Pride and Prejudice*, was in 1797 offered by her father to the publisher Thomas Cadell, who declined to see the manuscript. Before this setback she had started on a final version of another novel, which would become *Sense and Sensibility*. With their pictures of clever, sensitive sisters with not quite enough money and so a pressing but unacknowledged need to marry, both books seem to justify W. H. Auden's comic remarks:

> It makes me most uncomfortable to see
> An English spinster of the middle-class
> Describe the amorous effects of 'brass',
> Reveal so frankly and with such sobriety
> The economic basis of society.[9]

They also convey need for affection and respect in marriage and the subtle mutual love of siblings, all interacting with this 'economic basis'.

In 1801, in part to benefit his wife's health, George Austen appointed his son James as curate of Steventon, sold his farming lease, and proposed moving to Bath, where many water and electricity health treatments were on offer. There he, his wife, and two unmarried daughters could live comfortably in lodgings on the tithe income, which had appreciated during the last war-torn decade. Unconsulted about the decision, Jane is said to have fainted at the news, being, it is thought, appalled at the notion of separation from her childhood home, as well as the prospect of living in a crowded city.[10] Her letters of the time suggest a more ambivalent reaction. In January 1801, she wrote

> I get more & more reconciled to the idea of our removal. We have lived
> long enough in this Neighbourhood, the Basingstoke Balls are certainly
> on the decline, there is something interesting in the bustle of going away,
> & the prospect of spending future summers by the Sea or in Wales is
> very delightful . . . It must not be generally known however that I am not
> sacrificing a great deal in quitting the Country – or I can expect to
> inspire no tenderness, no interest, in those we leave behind.   (*L*, p. 68)

Her initial impression of the city that would be her home for the next five years is not recorded but in May 1801 she wrote to Cassandra that 'the first veiw of Bath in fine weather does not answer my expectations; I think I see more distinctly thro' Rain. – The sun was got behind everything, and the appearance of the place from the top of Kingsdown, was all vapour, shadow, smoke &

confusion' (*L*, p. 82). She had enjoyed the prospect of hunting for lodgings, although she soon tired of walking round unsuitable or 'putrifying' houses. Finally they rented in Sydney Place, moving three years later to Green Park Buildings East.

So little is known of the Bath period of Austen's life that speculation flourishes: she is portrayed sometimes as profoundly unhappy, at others as busy and involved, as falling in love or giving up all hope of love outside the family. Two startling facts stand out. When nearly twenty-seven, on a visit back to Hampshire, she accepted the proposal of a wealthy young man, Harris Bigg-Wither, whom a few hours later she rejected. Five years her junior, he was the heir of a considerable property in her Steventon neighbourhood and the brother of her good friends. Another interesting event occurred in spring 1803 when her skit on gothic writing, *Northanger Abbey*, then entitled 'Susan' and drafted probably in 1798–9, was sold for £10 to Benjamin Crosby & Co. The date suggests that Austen used the early part of her time in Bath to revise the third of the novels she had drafted in Steventon before the move. The book was not printed, however. Considering the level of much fiction published at the time it was a strange omission, caused, it has been surmised, by the astringency of the contents, although the practice of buying and delaying printing was not uncommon. Crosby had a financial interest in the popular gothic novelist Mrs Radcliffe and may not, on further thought, have wished to have her mocked in one of his productions.

About 1804 Austen began work on a new, harsher book, with more realistic touches than she had so far allowed herself. She wrote forty pages of *The Watsons*, graphically portraying the small humiliations involved in social sinking within a claustrophobic society. The story concerned four unmarried daughters of an ailing father with a small income: two are desperate husband-seekers, a third would be happy to remain single if she had an income, and a fourth, the more genteel Emma, returning from years spent with an affluent aunt, claims she would rather be a teacher than marry for money: later Emma was to have become dependent for 'a home on her narrow-minded sister-in-law and brother' (*FR*, p. 241). But, before Austen reached this point, she stopped writing. She did not return to the work, although it remained in her writing desk at her death, heavily corrected and not written out as a finished fair copy.

There are several possible reasons for her quitting. Since it occurred at about the time when she must have realised that 'Susan', like 'First Impressions' before it, was not going to be published, she might have felt demoralised. But, considering her later clear belief in the value of her writings, this is perhaps insufficient cause. Her nephew James Edward Austen-Leigh, who gave the novel its title, claimed she stopped because the subject matter was 'unfavourable to the refinement of a lady', being set in too lowly a rank of life where 'poverty and obscurity' may easily degenerate into 'vulgarity'. A further possibility, entwined with this social anxiety, is that Jane Austen abandoned *The Watsons* when her life turned upside down with her father's death (the father in the novel was also a cleric). The new financial and social precariousness may have upset the writing of a novel with a heroine in similarly reduced circumstances but younger in age. In her letters of the period there is considerable, if ironic, bitterness about money and status: 'prepare you[rself] for the sight of a Sister sunk in poverty, that it may not overcome your Spirits', she wrote to Cassandra (*L*, p. 108). The plot of *The Watsons* – a delicately brought-up girl returning to her poorer family and facing the threat of economic hardship – would recur in *Mansfield Park*.

When George Austen died early in 1805 his Steventon living passed to his son James; the living of Deane was now lost to the Austen family. Consequently the three women, with an annual income of £210 between them, including the interest on Cassandra's legacy from her dead fiancé, faced a life of dependence on the young male Austens: James, Henry, and Francis each contributed £50 per annum to their upkeep, Edward offered another £100. Without this support, their situation would not have been far from that of the Bates women in *Emma*, also widow and daughter of a country clergyman – or indeed the Watsons, who note 'Female Economy will do a great deal . . . but it cannot turn a small income into a large one.' The Austens gave up lodging in Green Park Buildings, and their friend Martha Lloyd, whose mother died three months after George, joined the household for both company and financial convenience. The arrangement was so successful that it continued for the next twenty years.

Between the death of George Austen in 1805 and Jane's arrival in Chawton in 1809 there is little evidence of creative activity. In summer 1806 the women travelled to Clifton near Bristol, from where they continued via Stoneleigh and Steventon to their journey's destination, Southampton, to set up house for a time in Castle Square with Jane's naval brother Francis and his new wife Mary. Whatever ambivalent feelings Jane had expressed about Bath on first arrival, she was glad not to return to the city: on 1 July 1808, she wrote 'It will be two years tomorrow since we left Bath for Clifton, with what happy feelings of Escape!' (*L*, p. 138). From Castle Square she made visits to Chawton Great House, Steventon, and her brother Henry's house in London; she also tasted luxury and ease for a few weeks at the mansion of Godmersham in Kent, owned by her brother Edward since 1798 (she visited less often than Cassandra, perhaps because this grand family was not entirely keen on a scribbling female relative). Whatever she was writing – and it is difficult to imagine her not writing – she emerged from these unsettled years a serious novelist with a wider range than she had commanded as a young girl in Steventon and, despite publishing setbacks, with a firm belief in her extraordinary talent.

In 1809, with expenses in Southampton rising, Mrs Austen, Jane, Cassandra, and Martha Lloyd were rescued by Edward, who, following the shock of his wife's death in October 1808 and the realisation that he was a widower with eleven children, offered his mother and sisters a free place to live in Chawton (now the Jane Austen museum): a cottage on the main road, with a flower and vegetable garden and pasturage for donkeys, situated close to his own extensive and often unoccupied manor. In this Hampshire village, never in want but never free from 'vulgar economy', the four women lived from then onwards a full family existence of visiting and being visited by siblings, nieces, and nephews.

Letters are full of trips to the country and London, where Jane went to parties, art galleries, and plays and indulged her fascination with dress and fashion, while grumbling over the exhausting shopping expeditions she made with her sister-in-law Eliza (although intensely interested in clothes, she was not keen on shopping for them). She never lost her enthusiasm for a city she once flippantly described as 'the Regions of Wit, Elegance, fashion, Elephants & Kangaroons' (*L*, p. 80).

In Chawton, despite the two publishing rebuffs, she began turning herself into a professional writer, joining the entrepreneurial intellectual classes burgeoning in the early nineteenth century.[11] From Southampton she had written to the publisher Crosby under the assumed name of Mrs Ashton Dennis, 'Authoress', stating that she assumed from the six-year delay in publishing that he had lost the manuscript of 'Susan' and suggesting she dispatch another copy. Crosby's son replied that she could have the manuscript back 'for the same as we paid for it' (*L*, pp. 174–5). She let the matter drop for the moment and began revising the other two Steventon drafts into *Sense and Sensibility* and *Pride and Prejudice*, the latter title possibly chosen because another fictional *First Impressions* (by Margaret Holford) had recently appeared in print. She was past the usual time of marriage and had 'taken to the garb of middle age' prematurely; if her financial and social position were to improve, it would have to be through what she did best, what alone seemed possible in her circumstances: writing for money.[12] Combined with a spinsterhood shared with congenial female companions, it was not an unattractive future.

The cancelled and rewritten chapters of *Persuasion* (the only surviving manuscript of a novel published in or just after Austen's lifetime) support her brother's claim that his sister needed 'many perusals' before she was satisfied. She was not a writer achieving perfection at once but one who needed to try, accept or change, score out and rewrite. Her critical and editorial abilities

equalled her creative; her judgement matched her inspiration. Kathryn Sutherland has rightly pointed out the simultaneity of Austen's new Chawton composition and her revision of the old, so that one novel will be gestating while
another is being corrected; taken together the six novels seem to 'enact a process
of expansion and repetition, retracing the old ground and discovering it as new
ground'.[13]

At the same time I find it striking that Austen could revise an early-conceived
novel and write a later one while keeping intact the individual stylistic integrity
of each. The Chawton novels – *Mansfield Park*, *Emma*, and *Persuasion* – continue to be romances ending in marriage, but they raise questions of identity
and responsibility, passion and selfhood that have no easy or definite answers,
often suggesting in their conclusion other trajectories than those they provide;
they leave a troubling sense of what might have been.

Much later her relatives and friends looked back on the Austen of the Chawton years. Although her works now seem less family affairs, more privately
authored, Cassandra recalled lively debates over drafts, for with her alone Jane
could talk 'freely of any work that she might have in hand'. Austen also discussed
strategies with her favourite nieces, knowing they would enter into her 'plea-
sures of Vanity'. Her nephew James Edward remembered an altogether more
'mystic process' of writing, disturbed by their childhood mischief which, as he
stressed, never elicited 'any signs of impatience or irritability' in their novelist
aunt (*FR*, p. 241; *Memoir*, p. 82). Meanwhile, Mary Russell Mitford repeated
her mother's unflattering surprise over the transformation Jane Austen had
undergone from the 'prettiest, silliest, most affected husband-hunting butter-
fly' to the author of *Mansfield Park*, 'stiffened into the most perpendicular,
precise, taciturn piece of "single blessedness" that ever existed'.[14]

Jane Austen entered the literary marketplace at a propitious time. Women
novelists had been increasing in number throughout the eighteenth century
and they actually formed a majority towards the end. Peter Garside has argued
that, by the 1810s, 'the *publication* of Jane Austen's novels was achieved not
against the grain but during a period of female ascendancy'; only in the 1820s
did male novelists become numerically dominant again – and then dominant
in the culture.[15] Austen was reading copiously in contemporary fiction by men
and women: as she wrote when replying to an invitation to subscribe to a library
boasting 'Literature' other than 'Novels', '*our* family . . . are great Novel-readers
& not ashamed of being so' (*L*, p. 26). Books were expensive and she knew from
her own experience – and to her cost as a writer – that readers were 'more ready
to borrow & praise, than to buy' (*L*, p. 287). She wanted to be an author who
was bought, read, and reread, whose books became both an experience and a
challenge to experience, not simply once-consumed items.

A writer could publish in four ways: sell the copyright and avoid further anxiety over production and sales; persuade a publisher to underwrite costs and share profits; get a subscription list to pay for publication, relying on friends, relatives, and patrons; or, less commonly, publish on commission, so paying for the book production, receiving profits minus a commission, and accepting any loss. In 1803 when 'Susan' had been offered to a publisher, Austen had tried the first option and had received the modest but usual sum of £10. In 1811 she tried the fourth when she sent *Sense and Sensibility* to Thomas Egerton, a London publisher, to be published on commission.

For this she may have borrowed from or used as guarantor her banking brother Henry, who wrote that she had saved money to cover costs should the novel not sell sufficiently to pay the expense of printing. Henry negotiated with the publisher and Jane came to London to correct proofs. Soon after her arrival Cassandra asked her about her progress, speculating that the enjoyments of town had put publishing out of her mind. 'No indeed', her sister replied, 'I am never too busy to think of S&S. I can no more forget it, than a mother can forget her sucking child' (*L*, p. 182). It was the culmination of fourteen years of trying to publish, and the novel being printed had had a gestation of sixteen.[16] When it appeared 'by a Lady', *Sense and Sensibility* received a couple of lukewarm reviews by critics liking its morality but surprised at its lack of sensational events. Ignorant of her aunt's involvement, James's daughter Anna declared it 'rubbish I am sure from the title' (*FR*, p. 191).

Despite this disappointing reception, the novel made money. The risk of commission-publishing had paid off and Jane Austen received £140. However, by the time she saw this, she had already sold the copyright of *Pride and Prejudice* for £110. She would rather have had £150, she wrote to Cassandra, but the quick transaction with Egerton 'will I hope be a great saving of Trouble to Henry' (*L*, p. 197); on 29 January 1813 she took delivery of her 'own darling Child' (*L*, p. 201). The publication affirmed her professional status by appearing as 'by the author of *Sense & Sensibility*'. *Pride and Prejudice* turned out to be Austen's most popular novel and the one that would have brought her most profit if published on commission.

She was excited by her limited success: together her two first works had earned £250, which, as she wrote to her brother Francis, 'only makes me long for more' (*L*, p. 217). Given her small income, the money obtained from publishing – all told between £600 and £700 – was clearly important, although the sum comes nowhere near the large amounts earned by Frances Burney – £4,000 for later editions of *Camilla* and *The Wanderer* – or Maria Edgeworth's £2,100 for *Patronage* and Hannah More's £2,000 in the first year for *Cœlebs in Search of a Wife*.

With *Mansfield Park*, Austen decided to try publication on commission again. Probably begun as she was sending *Sense and Sensibility* to the printers, this new work appeared in 1814 and she received the grand sum of £310, the most she would earn for any single novel. When Egerton delayed a second edition of what looked like a popular work – and perhaps because she was ambitious for a more important press – Austen moved to the fashionable John Murray II, publisher of the most celebrated writers of the day, Lord Byron and Walter Scott. Refusing his offer of £450 for the copyright of *Sense and Sensibility*, *Mansfield Park*, and her new novel, *Emma* (reluctantly dedicated to the 'hated' Prince Regent after he let her know through his librarian that he had her novels in both of his residences), she again insisted on commission publishing. Accepting that Murray was 'a rogue of course', she yet enjoyed his respectful address and was surprised at the expenses he passed on to her for advertising: he charged her £50 for promoting *Emma*, including in his own catalogue. When he brought out *Emma* together with a second edition of *Mansfield Park*, Austen lost so much on the latter that the former netted her only £39, despite being her largest first edition at 2,000 copies and despite its modest critical success. This was a blow, especially as it came in the same year in which her brother Henry's bank and army agency, heavily supported by his rich uncle James Leigh-Perrot and to a lesser extent by his brothers, failed, leaving Henry ruined – Jane lost about £25 from her profits (by 1816 her income from government stock was £30 per annum). As a direct result, both Henry and Francis could no longer afford the annual £50 each had contributed to their mother and sisters' upkeep.

These financial setbacks did not interfere with Austen's creativity or ambition. She had bought back her unpublished 'Susan' from Crosby, changed the heroine's name to Catherine and written a belligerent 'Advertisement' complaining of its neglect. But she found revision troubling: 'Miss Catherine is put upon the Shelve', she sighed, 'and I do not know that she will ever come out' (*L*, p. 333). The final title, *Northanger Abbey*, could have been hers or Henry's or Cassandra's, supplied when it was posthumously published. Meanwhile, she had finished, but not perhaps entirely revised, another novel; this too was posthumously named: *Persuasion*.

By now she was ill with a wasting disease – speculatively Addison's disease or possibly a lymphoma such as Hodgkin's disease.[17] Her illness was not helped by her uncle Leigh-Perrot's death, when it was disclosed that, despite his immense fortune, he had left all to his wife, and only after her death would his sister's children receive legacies: 'I am ashamed to say that the shock of my Uncle's Will brought on a relapse . . . I am the only one of the Legatees who has been so silly, but a weak Body must excuse weak Nerves' (*L*, p. 338). The blow came in the context of a lawsuit against her brother Edward which was threatening his ownership of the Chawton properties including the cottage; the lawsuit was settled only after her death.

Yet in January 1817 she had begun a new work, *Sanditon*, jovially mocking hypochondriacs (rather like her mother as she appears in Jane's letters) and depicting the self-indulgent performance illness could become. Her energetic invalid Diana Parker can hardly crawl from her 'Bed to the Sofa' and is 'bilious', a fashionable term superseding the earlier 'nervous', so effectively used by Mrs Bennet in *Pride and Prejudice*. This made a sufferer mottled and yellowish. Five days after abandoning the novel in its twelfth chapter, Austen wrote that she herself was turning 'every wrong colour' and living 'chiefly on the sofa' (*L*, pp. 335, 343). The few chapters of *Sanditon*, although much corrected, remain unfinalised. Yet, with its series of eccentrics and caricatures, reminiscent of her earlier novels, and its description not just of a deracinated family as in *Persuasion* but of a deracinated community (or 'a young & rising Bathing-place', as its promoter terms Sanditon), this briskly unsubtle book promised both continuity and development.

Jane Austen 'wrote whilst she could hold a pen, and with a pencil when a pen became too laborious'.[18] She herself made a note of the day she stopped writing *Sanditon*: 18 March 1817. In May she was taken to Winchester for treatment. Her illness was agony: as her sister reported, 'She said she could not tell us what she suffer'd.' She died in Winchester on 18 July. Her last spoken words expressed a desire for '*Nothing but death*' (*Memoir*, p. 131). Her last written ones were a poem on the effect of rain on St Swithin's day or, in her niece Caroline's phrase, a 'joke about the dead Saint and the Winchester races'. In this St Swithin, who has jumped on to the palace roof, declares: 'When once we are buried you think we are dead / But behold me immortal.'[19] Jane Austen was buried in Winchester Cathedral.

The vext nations

Jane Austen exists in our consciousness in a liminal historical space between the eighteenth and nineteenth centuries. Her period of publishing, 1811–17, coincides with the Regency period, when King George III's madness was considered permanent and his dissolute and unpopular son, later George IV, had become Prince Regent. This transitional time falls between revolutions: after the French Revolution, which had had such a profound political impact on Britain, and before the Industrial Revolution truly transformed the nation into the first urban industrial power.

Through almost all Jane Austen's adult life, Britain and France were at war. In the 1790s, when hostilities first began, the country was vulnerable and in danger, easy prey to the superior Revolutionary armies of expansionist France. With military failures abroad, the government feared French sympathisers within the kingdoms and responded by draconian measures: suspending *habeas corpus* and passing 'Gagging Acts' which banned public meetings. Yet many who were appalled at the French Terror of 1793–4 still held to reformist ideals and hoped that Britain could progress constitutionally and socially without following France into violence and dictatorship.

By the second decade of the nineteenth century, such hopes were largely dashed. The government's insistence on patriotism and control of print through taxes and regulations had made inroads into the Enlightenment reform movements and, with the Revolutionary and Napoleonic Wars dragging on, had impressed people who, decades earlier, would have seen such partiality as cant. The country had been blamed for losing its morale and will to win, and for failing to show the proper patriotism of moral principle and energetic enterprise. Meanwhile, the weariness of war was movingly expressed by writers such as Anna Laetitia Barbauld in her poem 'Eighteen Hundred and Eleven', which opened with the lament: 'Still the loud death drum, thundering from afar, / O'er the vext nations pours the storm of war.'

Two of Austen's brothers were in the Royal Navy, fighting the French. Francis joined Nelson in 1798 and helped pursue Napoleon after the Battle of the Nile; later he assisted in blockading the French fleet planning to invade Britain and accompanied convoys to Africa and the West Indies, narrowly missing the action at Trafalgar. Letters and newspapers kept Jane Austen in close contact with his and Charles's equally energetic wartime activities. She saw something of the fallout in men and money, but in her novels she allowed characters to feel pride in a new and assured maritime power and, even more, to revel in the entrepreneurial aspect of naval service, the possibility of prize money and advancement for the enterprising (officer) class: 'the glory of heroism, of usefulness, of exertion, of endurance', as Henry Crawford imagines it in *Mansfield Park*.

In 1814, Britain appeared to have won the war at sea and on land and Napoleon was exiled to Elba. Victory was celebrated throughout the country. Then, to national bewilderment, he escaped to France and recaptured Paris. As the journalist Leigh Hunt remarked, 'We want nothing now, to finish the romantic history of the present times, but a visit from the Man in the Moon.'[20] Renewed fighting followed and in June 1815 Wellington and the allies defeated Napoleon for the last time. Twenty-two years of war had really ended. Britain had become a major European and world power.

Disillusion soon followed victory, as the old order of kings and hierarchies was re-established in Europe. Returning warriors found themselves with little stake in the new Britain. Through the 1790s and early 1800s, despite the war and wartime blockades, the consumer boom for the well-off that had marked earlier decades continued. The result was a greater polarising of rich and poor: the former epitomised by the extravagant Prince of Wales and the gambling and drinking elite of London and fashionable watering holes; the latter by Luddites, impoverished workers who rebelled against machines designed to replace them and against enforced reduction of wages. When war ended in 1815, the ruling classes had little sense of how to cope with the problems of an increasingly divided and restless society and they responded to mass unemployment and the disastrous harvest of 1816 with stricter legislation. Their actions persuaded many that the ranks of society were no longer integrated but opposing.

From the six novels we may learn much of the political, spiritual, and intellectual attitudes available in Jane Austen's time. But she herself does not advocate positions so much as an enquiring mind: she sifts, queries, and explores issues rather than resolving them. The moral effect was brilliantly described in 1870 by Margaret Oliphant, who saw in Austen 'the soft and silent disbelief of a spectator who has to look at a great many things without showing any outward discomposure, and who has learned to give up any moral classification of social sins, and to place them instead on the level of absurdities'.[21] So, although she would have witnessed the beginnings of the capitalist agricultural and industrial transformation of Britain in rural Hampshire as well as the cities of London, Southampton, and Bath, she does not discuss society and politics at length and in abstract.[22]

Her earliest family biographers assumed she shared the Toryism of her clan, but her niece could not remember any political utterance her aunt made. The war with its effects features in the margins of the early novels, the neighbourhood spies of *Northanger Abbey* or the seductive militia of *Pride and Prejudice*, and it forms a more direct background to the final ones, emerging fully in *Persuasion*, coloured by the notion of conflict. Even here, however, there is no actual representation of war or its causes. The novels do not display a single political vision, and Austen cannot truly be labelled liberal, conservative, or moderate. Perhaps it would be fairer to call her multiply-minded, sometimes one, now the other, by turns or all together, or perhaps one might declare equivocality her predominant political mode. In her novels the kernel of life is outside politics, in love, affectionate duty, and sometimes sexual passion, threatened by selfishness and aggression, and she does not need to describe a national war or social upheaval directly to give a sense of the darkness on the edge of human existence. Yet the social and political resonance of national events just outside the frame helps prevent the complete closure of individual romance – the 'Tenderest & completest Eclaircissement' as her spoof 'Plan of a Novel' expresses it – and contributes to the wry melancholy of her happy endings.

The Church of England is a felt presence in Jane Austen's life. She was the Anglican daughter of an Anglican clergyman, presumed to hold traditional views on the role of the Church in society. These would encompass both piety and social realism: a man's entering the Church could result from vocation or simply family tradition and interest. Austen accepted the divine mission and implication of the Church but also its worldly function as a national institution. In this combining of religion with the politically useful she was not far from the Scottish divine and rhetorician Hugh Blair, whose book of *Sermons*, mentioned with some irony in 'Catharine' and with less by Mary Crawford in *Mansfield Park*, was one of the age's most read and appreciated works.

Austen's distaste for the new movement of Evangelicalism (an enthusiastic tendency which emphasised conversion and an entirely different life in Christ, while seeking to interrupt the lax social harmony of the established Church) is boldly expressed in 1809 to Cassandra, 'I do not like the Evangelicals' (*L*, p. 170). By 1814, the year of *Mansfield Park*'s publication, however, she had qualified her distaste: 'I am by no means convinced that we ought not all to be Evangelicals'; she was 'at least persuaded that they who are so from Reason & Feeling, must be happiest & safest' (*L*, p. 280). In the most ominous years of the Napoleonic War she had come to value Evangelicalism's seriousness, its implied critique of the triviality of many Anglican members and ministers. Yet her final two novels do not continue the critique, and the (equivocal) social ideal apparently vested in serious clergymen in *Mansfield Park* settles on working gentleman farmers in *Emma* and entrepreneurial sailors in *Persuasion*. Austen seems to have professed in her novels the kind of morality that grew from the accepted doctrines of the Church of England – that human nature is always fallible, and that pain and difficulties help to create a soul – but her books are not primarily religious ones like those of Hannah More and Jane West: they may show affliction but do not preach the need for it.

Similarly, she is not primarily a philosophical writer. The attitudes and vocabulary of the British Enlightenment thinkers, from Locke to her contemporary Adam Smith, were in the atmosphere breathed by intelligent bookish people like the Austens. Jane Austen does not so much engage intellectually with the works of the philosophers, the Earl of Shaftesbury, Adam Smith, and David Hume, as use them within her novels in parodic or allusive ways to reveal her characters.[23] In tone she seems closest to Hume, whose historical writings she admired. Hume argued against moral absolutes and for the importance of context and difference in any judgement; like other Enlightenment thinkers he stressed the value of ordinary existence. Austen, too, was pragmatic about human nature, seeing it less fixed than subject to circumstances. She may have felt 'Composition . . . Impossible' with 'a head full of Joints of Mutton & doses of rhubarb' (*L*, p. 321); yet she was a writer who had a sharp eye for the everyday matter of existence. In this study I will connect Hume's pragmatic philosophical and psychological writings with Austen's works when appropriate.

Jane Austen's novels are experimental. Each presents a different sort of heroine, a different take on society and the relationship of behaviour and personality to environment, a different sort of investigation, almost a different moral message, if one can here use so unnuanced a word. One book will describe a situation and treat it in a particular way, the next will give quite a different outcome. The flattery that destroys Maria of *Mansfield Park* will not much harm the heroine of *Emma*, while Maria's harsh fate is not shared by Lydia in *Pride and Prejudice*, although her indecent act is similar. Appearing simple and superficially repetitive, the plots are in fact innovative in their tightness, their insistence that every incident and character serve the onward thrust. Equally experimental are the openings: the slow circumstantial family settings of *Sense and Sensibility*, *Mansfield Park*, and *Persuasion*, a parodic take on this convention in *Northanger Abbey*, a fast-paced plunge into marital bickering in *Pride and Prejudice*, and a sudden glimpse of the heroine's consciousness in *Emma*.

When Emma declares that Harriet must be a gentleman's daughter, the Austen reader is reminded of Elizabeth's proud boast in *Pride and Prejudice*, truncated when Lady Catherine alludes to her mother, while Emma's defensive remark that 'A man always imagines a woman to be ready for anybody who asks her' (*E*, 1:8) echoes the heroine's intense response to Sir Thomas in *Mansfield Park* as he presses her into an unwanted marriage. The two statements are differently inflected and yet both come from young women who are in some way mentally isolated. The echoes and dialogue across novels increase the comedy and complexity, while suggesting other possibilities of feeling and action. They add to an impression of fluidity, implying that there is no single secure moral or socio-political vision that cannot be investigated, a little ironised, or a little mocked.

Chapter 2

The literary context

Where many aspiring writers begin by expressing their disgust with the adult world of parents or by picturing a compensatory fantasy life, Jane Austen started with mimicry and parody, writing burlesques and pastiches of grown-up fiction and reading them aloud to her family. In the last year of her life she wrote to a niece that she wished she had written less and read more when a child, but the habit of close stylistic scrutiny which parody requires stood her in excellent stead. It is a measure of her present power that almost single-handedly she has made most of her contemporaries seem excessive, artificial, or absurd.

I must keep to my own style

No one could intend to be a serious novelist in the late eighteenth century without being aware of the genre of fiction and without thinking of the great male forebears, Samuel Richardson and Henry Fielding. As their successor, Jane Austen was ambivalent about their achievements. Richardson was considered the major originator of women's fiction: his novels *Pamela* (1740) and *Clarissa* (1747–8) have central female characters and much of the interest of *Sir Charles Grandison* (1753–4) inheres in the women. All three novels are written in letters, so displaying not so much the inner consciousness of characters as their self-analyses, their sense of their own conscience, and their self-projection. The young women confront moral and social questions, and struggle to assert themselves in an alien world mainly through the act of writing. (Here Austen contrasts with Richardson since her concern is primarily *reading*; where his works display the paraphernalia of pen, ink, paper and codes, hers are full of novels and newspapers).

Richardson's writing – and literary success – was closely tied to the cultural phenomenon of 'sensibility', one of the major topics of eighteenth-century literature and philosophy. Appropriated and mocked by both conservative and radical thinkers at different moments in the 1780s and '90s, 'sensibility' bore on all aspects of human nature and society. It stressed spontaneous emotion and expression, assuming innate virtue in the undamaged individual rather than an essentially erring human nature needing external rules (and religion). Associated particularly with women, it spoke through the body, deemed to be authentic in its palpable expression of feeling, and it could easily promote frailty, even sickness, in those regarding themselves as excessively sensitive and virtuous.

'Sympathy', the spontaneous human ability to participate imaginatively in the happiness and pain of another, was the fundamental and largely undisputed foundation of the ideology. The power of sympathy was prized for its individual and social influence: according to the poet James Thomson, it was the prerogative of man over other animals that nature had taught him to weep.[1] The human capacity for sympathy formed a basis for social relations and moral attitudes: David Hume's *A Treatise of Human Nature* (1739–40) described a sociability grounded in the mobility of passions which transcended the principle of self-interest propounded by earlier thinkers like Thomas Hobbes and Bernard Mandeville. Hume's concept was strengthened by medical research into the nervous system, most importantly Robert Whytt's *Observations on the Nature, Causes and Cure of the Diseases which are commonly called Nervous, Hypochondriac or Hysteric* (1764). This work studied physical acts such as laughter or crying that can be excited in another and provided physiological evidence to support a moral theory that it was 'through sympathy that human beings are basically able to communicate with each other'.

Working as it does through mechanisms of spectatorship, reader identification and response, literature proved an ideal vehicle for sentimental ideology. Presenting examples of affective conduct, novels of sensibility produced norms: moral values promoted within the narratives – charity towards the poor, empathy with the less fortunate – were to be re-enacted by readers in their own lives. In the process, novels themselves became touchstones for that morality. A reader's appropriate feeling response to the fictive spectacle of suffering was deemed the natural result of his or her ethics. Richardson's spun-out story of feminine virtue betrayed and violated was a benchmark of sentimental writing – Clarissa's heartfelt language pulsed with the fluctuations of her extreme emotion, conveyed through hyperbole, staccato syntax, and a liberal use of exclamations: 'Oh my best, my only friend! Now indeed is my heart broken! – It has received a blow it never will recover!' (Letter 146).

According to Henry Austen, his sister hugely admired Richardson, especially *Sir Charles Grandison*. Reference to it spans her writing life. In *Northanger Abbey*, Richardson's novel is much appreciated by the worthy but unimaginative Mrs Morland, while in *Sanditon*, the foolishly susceptible Sir Edward Denham is inspired by 'all the impassioned, and most exceptionable parts of

Richardson' which portray 'Man's determined pursuit of Woman in defiance of every opposition of feeling & convenience'. The most tedious of the novels, *Sir Charles Grandison* led Austen to imagine a more succinct fiction existing with little plot yet much nuance of feeling, one which communicated through a language that conveyed intensity without having recourse to Richardson's excess – the best examples of which are surely her late works *Emma* and *Persuasion*. At the same time, Richardson's investigation of aspects of passionate subjectivity taught her much of what the novel might do.

In the gendered critical structure of the eighteenth century Fielding was the masculine writer to Richardson's feminine. In his novels, especially *Joseph Andrews* (1742) and *Tom Jones* (1749), Fielding combined rollicking tales of manly sexual adventure with a self-consciousness about genre and a sense of the literariness of fiction. Beginning as a skit on Richardson's *Pamela*, *Joseph Andrews* brought parody and burlesque into serious narrative. Regardless of whether she indeed 'recoiled' from Fielding's 'so very low a scale of morals', as her brother claimed (*Memoir*, p. 141), Jane Austen may have learned from his work. She could have noted not only the power of parody but also the combination of third-person narration with an intrusive opinionated narrator, now omniscient, now mock-omniscient, who influences and distorts the story and allows multiple readings. When Austen was brought forward primarily as a serious literary writer and fictional innovator in the early to mid-twentieth century, she was placed in the tradition of these male predecessors: both F. R. Leavis and Ian Watt saw Richardson and Fielding as parenting Austen, who combined their qualities of interiority and irony, realism and satire to form an author superior to both.

At much the same time Mary Lascelles argued that Jane Austen had trained herself in Samuel Johnson's school, improving through him her aptitude for pregnant abstraction and antithetic phrasing.[2] Austen acknowledged a connection, apologising to her sister over a letter lacking proper subject – 'like my dear Dr Johnson I beleive I have dealt more in Notions than Facts' (*L*, p. 121). Johnson, the foremost literary moralist, essayist, and lexicographer of the eighteenth century, was famed for his precise grammar, measured prose, balanced syntax, and generalisation, which, when not interrupted by wit and unexpected antithesis, often bordered on the sententious. The style is rooted in ethics, and Austen's moral lexicon of general abstract terms such as 'manners', 'duty', and 'good-breeding', reflects a Johnsonian belief that society agreed on their distinct meaning within a universal standard (in fact the terms were by no means as vague then as they now seem). However, despite its closeness, Austen's narrative style possesses greater flexibility than Johnson's prose: she balanced formal moral observation with commonplace and often inconsequential dialogue, and nuanced moral statements with ironic distance, so avoiding the pompous and unequivocal.

With the development of feminist criticism in the 1970s, Jane Austen came more into the company of other women, especially of Frances Burney, whose novels of manners, particularly *Evelina* (1778), *Cecilia* (1782), and *Camilla* (1796), depict the adventures of young ladies with good principles but little understanding of the 'world'. They enter society and learn to behave in a 'well-bred' way and to separate the false from the genuine; in the process of being trained, often almost to death, they find true love, usually with the man who has been their mentor or model – and sometimes tormentor. Austen certainly avails herself of this entry plot, but she uses it more subtly than the often didactic and sensational Burney. She allows her heroines' moments of discovery to emerge from ordinary events within a normal everyday world, where Burney's young women are routinely subjected to extreme experiences of social and sexual disgrace, madness and death, which bring them close to psychological collapse before they are allowed to discover their errors.

Through *Evelina*, Burney presses most heavily on the Bath section of *Northanger Abbey*. Both Catherine, Austen's heroine, and Evelina arrive in a new society under the wing of an inadequate chaperone and, despite good hearts and correct principles, make mistakes of etiquette. They are constantly misrepresented and manipulated into indecorous behaviour until they learn how to fulfil and use social conventions; then they marry the heroes, men of consummate social and intellectual skill – and in Burney's case a lord. In the context of this resemblance, Austen can mock her predecessor, contrasting her own plain and ignorant heroine with Burney's angelically beautiful and accomplished Evelina, whose éclat on the dance floor puts into the shade Catherine's modest effect. When the hero Henry Tilney playfully insists Catherine must keep a journal, he is comparing her with Evelina, who writes copious and detailed accounts of every aspect of her life, and, when Catherine assumes her friend must look exactly like her dead mother, she echoes the convention which makes the beautiful Evelina identical with her beautiful mother.

The harangues and chidings given by the Burney male mentors to the slightly erring heroines are echoed in the reproaches of Austen's heroes,[3] but in Austen's novels their targets are never completely reformed by instruction (and instructors are usually in need of some improvement themselves); moments of self-recognition come rather from the heroines' own experience. When Catherine or Emma thinks she is utterly changed by a rebuke, the narrator pokes gentle fun at her, for morality is not a single response but a constant struggle to understand and discriminate.

Unlike the women's novels that immediately followed the polarised years after the French Revolution – Mary Wollstonecraft's or Mary Hays's or those of the earnest and Christian Mary Brunton, Jane West, Hannah More, or Laetitia Matilda Hawkins – Austen's do not insist on a didactic goal, whether politically radical or Christian, usually at the expense of probability. When More's widely read but much criticised educative novel *Cœlebs* appeared, Austen wrote to Cassandra: 'You have by no means raised my curiosity after Caleb; – My disinclination for it before was affected, but now it is real' (*L*, p. 170) and later she described Brunton's *Self-Control* as 'excellently-meant, elegantly-written' and 'without anything of Nature or Probability in it' (*L*, p. 234). In 1814 she declared herself 'stout against any thing written by Mrs West' (*L*, p. 278) and the following year called Hawkins's overtly Christian *Rosanne* (1814) 'clever' but 'tedious' (*L*, p. 289).

Whatever serious project Austen attempted, she would never make a direct and unremitting assault on the reader, and her heroines would not be 'Morality's prim personification'.[4] She remained a private consumer of sermons and moral exhortations but not a writer of them. Characters (and readers) who think literature, even advice writing, can be applied directly to life are mocked. The ending of *Northanger Abbey* declares, 'I leave it to be settled by whomsoever it may concern, whether the tendency of this work be altogether to recommend parental tyranny, or reward filial disobedience' (*NA*, 2:16). That Austen conveyed moral enquiry without being didactic was what struck her best earliest critics. It was the passionate core in the novels that prevented didacticism according to Richard Whately, who wrote in the *Quarterly Review* for January 1821 that, although she was 'evidently a Christian writer', she provided no 'dramatic sermon': her characters are not 'fiends or angels' and even the worthiest like Fanny Price in *Mansfield Park* is shown to be under 'the influence of strong passion, [which] must alloy the purest mind, but with which scarcely any *authoress* but Miss Austin would have ventured to temper the aetheriel materials of a heroine'.[5]

In the hands of Burney and her successors, the novel of a woman's entry into society lent itself to discussions of female education, often with dire portraits of faulty upbringing. Education was a current cultural concern of the turbulent late eighteenth century, freighted with ideology and comprising both formal training and the fitting of a child for its proper social place. Cultural anxiety expressed itself in the flourishing of a genre known as the conduct book. Advice books had always existed, but the large number aimed at gentry and middle-class girls was a phenomenon of the revolutionary and transitional period of the late eighteenth and early nineteenth centuries. These works preached traditional feminine values of prudence, modesty, and contingence and stressed Christian seriousness and restraint; keeping the focus firmly on marriage, they also advised a girl to hide any wit or learning she might possess and avoid improper physical display. Austen's most succinct comment on conduct books is the portrait of the oily and absurd Mr Collins of *Pride and Prejudice*, who appears to have learnt about women and their attitudes entirely from them. In *Northanger Abbey* the heroine remains untouched by conduct-book instruction; a commonsensical and virtuous family do much to form her and so does her natural propensity to ignore feminine affectation and, as a child, to roll down grassy green slopes.

Many women novelists, both conservative like Hannah More and Jane West, liberal like Elizabeth Inchbald and Maria Edgeworth, or more radical like Mary Wollstonecraft and Mary Hays, mocked the impoverished training in accomplishments (dancing, sketching, music, and fancy needlework, 'frivolity and trifles' in Hays's words) provided for middle- and upper-class girls by governesses and boarding schools and aimed primarily at catching a husband. Such education led to 'perpetual childhood', indiscipline, sexual fixation, boredom, and, if not corrected by harsh experience, lifelong unhappiness.[6] Austen joins her sister writers in mocking it – especially when provided for girls below the gentry rank: in her juvenile 'Jack and Alice, A Novel', a girl describes how, 'first-rate Masters . . . taught me all the accomplishments requisite for one of my sex and rank. Under their instructions I learned Dancing, Music, Drawing & various Languages, by which means I became more accomplished than any other Taylor's Daughter in Wales.' In 'Catharine or the Bower', the frivolous Camilla Stanley is ridiculed for spending twelve years of education on drawing and music-making. In *Emma*, Mrs Elton celebrates her marriage by putting away her music, for its purpose has been accomplished, while the head teacher of the local boarding school spends time collecting riddles.

Yet Austen does not follow authors like Wollstonecraft into proposing more rigorous and rational education, whether delivered through formal schooling or controlled reading, and in *Pride and Prejudice* she ridicules the intellectual ambition of Mary Bennet. In *Mansfield Park*, the Bertram daughters can put the map of Europe together, tell the principal rivers of Russia and recite the chronological order of the kings of England and Roman emperors, 'besides a great deal of the Heathen Mythology, and all the Metals, Semi-Metals, Planets, and distinguished philosophers' (*MP*, 1:2), but they lack principles and any sense of duty. Elizabeth Bennet achieves both despite a silly mother and no governess, and Emma increases in understanding while her reading lists remain unread. Austen rejected the views of her more utopian contemporaries, that education including environment could determine development and character and so engineer an earthly paradise.

A fictional genre which, in women's hands, often meshed with sentimental and didactic novels from which Jane Austen learned much, while judging it amusingly absurd, was the gothic. This was popular throughout her life, but most influential in the violent decade of the 1790s. Afterwards, although it continued to be written and read – peaking in about 1810 – it was attacked on literary and political grounds as pandering to the kind of sensationalism that produced disorder in the individual and the state.

Austen's *Juvenilia* made fun of those sensational tabooed subjects which gothic writers, such as Horace Walpole, Matthew Lewis, and Charlotte Dacre, treated explicitly and the more decorous and skilled Ann Radcliffe touched on. As a mature writer she wrote of subjects far removed from Radcliffe's extravagant adventures and exotic locations, but she could derive from her predecessor the gothic techniques of suspense – how to keep a reader reading. If her books do not make hair stand on end in the way Henry Tilney described Radcliffe's doing, they keep readers guessing and waiting, eager to move to the next volume, persuaded for the moment to live in the fictional world. This is what Radcliffe above all had achieved and Austen dramatised it in the portrait of Catherine Morland in *Northanger Abbey*. By the time she wrote *Emma* and gave gothic reading to the silly Harriet and not the hero, she respected its power less clearly, although still using its techniques.

Radcliffe was the best of a mass of gothic writers who benefited from the eighteenth-century change in reading habits. In his essay 'Of the Rise and Progress of the Arts and Sciences' (1742) David Hume noted, 'You will never want booksellers while there are buyers of books', and the circulating libraries were serviced by new, fast-paced commercial publishers like William Lane of the Minerva Press.[7] Together with the libraries, such presses created a new kind of consumer who borrowed, read fast, and exchanged or passed on books, in contrast to those who bought expensively, kept, and reread. But Austen, although needing to exploit circulating libraries, wrote against the commercial trend. She did not claim, like some Romantic poets, that she was writing primarily for posterity rather than the present frivolous public, but she did want readers prepared to read more than once and to look for something beyond the plot. Her letters reveal that she read even feeble books several times before pronouncing on them and that she encouraged frequent readings of her manuscripts by her family.

Austen was publishing in the era of the Romantic poets, of Scott, William Wordsworth, Robert Southey, and Byron. She was fully aware of the new literary scene and her references in her later novels are less to Radcliffe, Burney, and Cowper than to Byron and Scott. In *Persuasion* she alluded openly to Byron's *Turkish Tales* and Scott's *Lady of the Lake* and *Marmion*. After the publication of the very successful *Waverley* in 1814, which fictionalised the Jacobite Rebellion of 1745, she knew that Scott had become the dominant fiction writer in Britain. 'It is not fair', she joked, 'He has Fame & Profit enough as a Poet, and should not be taking the bread out of other people's mouths' (*L*, p. 277). Scott had replaced the high gothic of Radcliffe with historical romance, using more realistic detail and psychology and providing some accurate historical facts. Where the gothic with its fearsome exotic Catholicism had ministered to Protestant religious nationalism, Scott (like Edgeworth and Sydney Owenson for Ireland) served the political nationalistic interests both of Scotland and of the United Kingdom, while making the Celtic periphery exotic for an English audience. Although from the late nineteenth century Austen has been associated with Englishness, she herself found national epics not to her taste. In *Persuasion* her passing references to recent events may have been influenced by Scott (or be a similar response to cultural ambience), but her apprehension of history remains more ironic and oblique than his: the Napoleonic War arrives through the hero's almost bragging accounts of partly mercenary naval engagements and, in the central consciousness of the heroine, is transformed into an ambiguous private patriotism.

When the Prince Regent's librarian, James Stanier Clarke, suggested she might try writing 'any Historical Romance illustrative of the History of the august house of Cobourg' (*L*, p. 311) to please the royal family and presumably combine moral uplift with fashionable romantic nationalism, Austen replied,

> I could no more write a Romance than an Epic Poem. – I could not sit seriously down to write a serious Romance under any other motive than to save my Life, & if it were indispensable for me to keep it up & never relax into laughing at myself or other people, I am sure I should be hung before I had finished the first Chapter. – No – I must keep to my own style & go on in my own Way; And though I may never succeed again in that, I am convinced that I should totally fail in any other.

She declared her forte to be 'pictures of domestic Life in Country Villages' (*L*, p. 312); it was left to the Scottish Jane Porter to fulfil the royal requirement with *Duke Christian of Luneberg, or Traditions of the Hartz* (1824).

Nature or probability

Austen's novels are hybrids, romance and comedy, satire and sentiment, fairy tale and realism. Despite verisimilitude in conversation and character, the conclusions of the novels remain romantic: marriage of the correct couple against

odds or opposition (often from within themselves) and the resulting better-
ment of the community. Plain girls become beauties and get their loves once
they are properly noticed by the heroes, and witty couples settle into genteel
domesticity. The obsession, misery, erotic passion, and jealousy, which, along
with manners and social jostling, form the subject matter, echo themes in
folklore where girls are woken from seeming death and the least likely third
girl gets the prince. The hybridity of romance and realism diminishes neither:
accepting romantic closure the novels avoid intellectual closure, so allowing a
reader to continue thinking. Meanwhile, despite this cerebral appeal, they have
made the Regency period almost synonymous with modern popular notions
of romance.

Samuel Johnson argued:

> All joy or sorrow for the happiness or calamities of others is produced by
> an act of the imagination, that realizes the event however fictitious, or
> approximates it however remote, by placing us, for a time, in the
> condition of him whose fortunes we contemplate; so that we feel, while
> the deception lasts, whatever emotions would be excited by the same
> good or evil happening to ourselves.[8]

Eighteenth-century readers thought of Richardson's Pamela and Clarissa outside the novels and identified with them, but Austen is the first novelist whose
central characters now live for *modern* readers as men and women with whom
they can identify and about whom they might fantasise.[9] Even when the narrator distances or gently mocks the reader for accepting the heroines as 'real',
it is hard to give up the belief, as numerous sequels and recreations testify.
Jane Austen's skill at suggesting a reality beyond the novel is playfully declared
when she herself indicated afterlives: Miss Steele of *Sense and Sensibility* 'never
succeeded in catching the Doctor'; Mr Woodhouse in *Emma* would prevent
his daughter and Mr Knightley from settling at Donwell for another two years,
while delicate Jane Fairfax would outlive him a mere seven years (*Memoir*,
p. 119; *FR*, p. 241). While visiting London in 1813, Austen claimed she was
looking for pictures of her characters among the miniatures shown at the Society of Painters' display; she was pleased 'particularly' with 'a small portrait
of Mrs Bingley' declaring 'there never was a greater likeness'. Mrs Darcy was,
however, not to be found at any of the exhibitions and she assumed her husband would 'prize[] any Picture of her too much' to wish it shown publicly (*L*,
pp. 212–13).

Readers have always known that mimesis is a mirage and that characters
are a textual effect, while believing in their 'reality'. Jane Austen plays with
this complex belief within as well as outside the novels; in *Northanger Abbey*,

while giving the heroine many realistic traits and letting us into her inner life, she allows the intrusive narrator to prevent identification – even as she lets us occasionally fall into an equally comic sense of the narrator as 'real' representing the 'real' world. At the close, when she is loudly insisting that we are reading fiction and should know it by now, that it would be absurd to believe in a fictive world in which all details are summarily connected, she swerves aside to assert that the story is life by insisting on her own joy at the good Eleanor Tilney's timely marriage – which fictional convention has brought about. In *Mansfield Park* she destabilises our suspension of disbelief by speculating that Sir Thomas 'might perhaps' not be amused to have his supine wife as card partner.

Many critics have considered how Austen achieves her illusion of character through mere words, what rhetorical strategies she uses to represent the inner life and deliver as 'realistic' an intimacy with another unachievable in 'real' life. One technique is by reproducing in fiction what David Hume calls the psychological habit of 'projection'. In *Pride and Prejudice*, for example, Jane and Elizabeth Bennet (wrongly) imagine in their wild sister Lydia the emotions they would feel had they themselves erred and been rescued. Reader identification works along similar lines: Deidre Shauna Lynch suggests that in this period 'character reading was reinvented as an occasion when readers found themselves and plumbed their own interior resources of sensibility by plumbing characters' hidden depths'.[10]

Further realism is given by the heroines' possession of memory, sometimes seen by the reader to be faulty in its operation, and by a habit of acting accord- ing to dimly understood or admitted motives and impulses springing from their past or from family inheritance. In *Northanger Abbey*, the ebullient role- playing hero only slowly reveals to the reader the scars of a home life marked by pretence and repression. Hume had destabilised knowledge and memory by deriving both from original sense impressions and arbitrary personal asso- ciations. Austen's characters are made to discover the instability of their most cherished beliefs and memories: when Elizabeth Bennet starts to doubt her good opinion, even love, of Wickham, she finds that her remembrance of his mental and physical charm dissolves.

Memory includes what has been read and learnt, words that inhabit the mind. The characters rarely discuss literary works at length but quotations, banally or seriously assimilated, lodge there and become part of mental fur- niture, moved to the fore voluntarily or involuntarily. They are influenced by books which may unconsciously infiltrate their ways of thinking; at other times they will consciously appropriate literary or fictional language to serve social or emotional ends. Marianne's compulsive reading shapes her man- ner and outlook on the world; when experience alters her, she changes her books. Facing a romantic crisis, both she and Emma find comfort in intended reading.

Despite emphasis on an inner and bodily life, the heroines fully inhabit the external world; they participate in hackneyed dialogues and react casually to what others say. They do not usually declaim; rather they interrupt and move about, respond, quiz, flirt, and grow suddenly preoccupied in the midst of talk. The heroines are aware of the play of social codes and conventions: they reflect on them and use them to communicate. Indeed the role-playing of much social life is so noticed in the novels that we start to assume a contrasting authenticity within the central characters.

In short, throughout the novels the heroine's interior consciousness is presented as interactive with her physical being, cultural influences, and external forces. Austen presents this consciousness in such a way that we believe we penetrate through the exterior into the inner life, gaining a sense of this life pressing against an outside world and changing with circumstances. There is none of the lengthy public self-analysis and introspection of, for example, Clarissa – and little of the self-absorption that marks heroines of later novels such as *Jane Eyre* or Virginia Woolf's *Mrs Dalloway;* instead there is interaction between thought and speech, private and social selves. The characters read other characters and their surroundings: despite the distancing through an often ironic, incorporeal yet strangely substantial narrator, they seem 'real' to the reader because they, like readers, are watchers of others, second-guessers, puzzlers of texts, while imagining people outside themselves.

Despite some resemblance in inner–outer interaction, the main characters are unlike the self-obsessed heroes of Romantic poetry.[11] They are not weighed down by a sense of themselves struggling against an almost abstract entity called Society but are part of what they analyse and sometimes disapprove. The egotistical solitary image in Wordsworth's *Prelude* contrasts with the more sociable Romanticism of the second generation of Romantics, Shelley, Keats, and Leigh Hunt, but the visionary narcissism of the latter group still aims at making society in its own image. With minimal description, Austen's heroines are embedded in time, place, and fashion; they are endowed with plausible modes of speaking and looking, and given suitable phrases, hairstyles, and clothes.[12] They search for picturesque views and go to tourist spots to see what they are supposed to see. Inhabiting a domestic world of drawing rooms and parks, they are rarely totally alone, although they may retreat like any Romantic poet to gain a sense of themselves. Often their seclusion is invaded, as Fanny's East Room is in *Mansfield Park* or Elizabeth's solitary walk at Rosings. In this their situation mirrors the author's (in the now traditional picture of her). Austen wrote in a substantial material world, realised for readers of her life in the details from Chawton cottage: the creaking swing door which, according to her nephew, 'gave her notice when anyone was coming' and the 'piece of blotting paper' which allowed her to hide her manuscript sheets from prying eyes (*Memoir*, pp. 81–2). The Austen in this picture does not need to take opium like Coleridge or climb Snowdon with Wordsworth. Neither she nor her characters accept the nineteenth century's estrangement of the writer from the material world of labour and things. Her most imaginative character, Emma, lives among pencil stubs, court plaster, apples, and gruel.

Little bit (two Inches wide) of Ivory

Characters exist among other people. They are separate consciousnesses within social spaces often trying to link through language with other consciousnesses. The books investigate through words and investigate words; they are about conversation that forms an exchange of opinion and feeling, about phrases that inhabit people's brains and make the timbre of their minds, about 'commonplace foolishness' and about the trivial remarks that assume immense significance.[13] Although she took much from the theatre – from the alternate fainting on the sofa of 'Love & Freindship' and the numerous 'starts' of surprised characters to the interruption of a theatrical rant by a more naturalistic mode in *Mansfield Park* – Austen's dialogue is not altogether theatrical, as adapters of her novels discover when they try directly to transfer her wit from page to stage. Speech in fiction can be more succinct than in the theatre, more a summary of conversations.

Jane Austen was well aware of the difference between drama and prose fiction. As a child she enjoyed plays put on in the Steventon barn such as Richard Brinsley Sheridan's comedy *The Rivals*, Thomas Francklin's melodramatic tragedy *Matilda*, and Isaac Bickerstaffe's farce *The Sultan*.[14] She noted that Shakespeare permeates everyone's mind; he also permeates her novels: *A Midsummer Night's Dream* hangs over *Mansfield Park*, whose erotically subjected characters wander through woods loving the wrong people, while *The Tempest* and *A Winter's Tale* come close to *Persuasion* with its enchantments and romantic elegiac mood. Beyond theatre there was much communal reading aloud of novels, so that Austen would early on have had a dramatic sense of written dialogue, something between ordinary and theatrical speech; she herself read with 'great taste and effect' (*Memoir*, p. 140) and enjoyed (and benefited from) the critical interaction of the reading group. In part as a result of this training her dialogue strikes readers as more 'natural' than that of other early nineteenth-century novelists: the protagonists do not declaim but frequently exchange brief prosaic remarks not always freighted with meaning and significance. The novels are full of conversational encounters in which neither participant listens to the other.

In her mimicry of idiosyncratic speech Austen learned much from Frances Burney, whose delight in odd verbal habits and the jargons of trade and fashion she shared. But more than Burney she enjoyed the 'nothing-saying' of talk, the hum of ready-made, prefabricated language that smooths everyday intercourse for good or ill and is almost communal, as in this depiction of the Donwell strawberry expedition in *Emma*:

> Morning decidedly the best time – never tired – every sort good – hautboy infinitely superior – no comparison – the others hardly eatable – hautboys very scarce . . . tired to death – could bear it no longer – must go and sit in the shade.   (*E*, 3:6)

Related to represented dialogue is a technique with which Austen is peculiarly associated: she was the '[f]irst author to grasp fully the technique of using free indirect discourse to represent the *lived* self in the moment'.[15] Free indirect speech is a technique on the cusp between speech and narratorial discourse; it is employed in passages usually without quotation marks which are not delivered as direct speech but which represent characters' expression by employing their vocabulary, phrases, sentence structure, and idiomatic inflections. Direct and indirect speech, subjectivity and objectivity merge, and the narrator, allowing distance from the character, mimics her style. When used for the central consciousness, the reader both identifies with this consciousness and suspects it is not necessarily authoritative; what is delivered may be point of view rather than objective fact.

Employed with a knowing but not all-knowing fictional narrator, free indirect speech can appear ironic, as it does frequently in *Northanger Abbey*. In the later novels the effect is most complex, for example with the sympathetic but deluded Emma, who reflects that her friend 'had a sweet, docile, graceful disposition', while 'strength of understanding [was] not [to] be expected', although her 'early attachment to herself was very amiable' and 'shewed that there was no want of taste' (*E*, 1:4). Here Emma is revealed as clever, vain, anxious, and manipulative all at the same time. Subconsciously, she is imagining the ideal wife a man wants, one she knows is far from herself, and revealing her relish for power, her selfish use of another for her own ends. At other times, used for a more inward heroine, the device gives an intimacy, a sense of an inner life, as in Anne Elliot's anguish over her beloved Wentworth: 'Once so much to each other! Now nothing!' (*P*, 1:8). Often it will occur when the heroine is reading a letter or thinking about an action or watching others. Apart from indicating deep feeling or anxious discriminating, it allows her to make errors and judge wrongly without the narrator condemning or patronising her or the reader.

The Austen narrator is a strange presence. Many readers end the novels with a sense of an author behind the acerbic, sharpish commentator as well as the assertive heroines: not an author like Charlotte Brontë, whom Virginia Woolf blames for intruding personally into *Jane Eyre*, but one who through the narrator colludes with the reader and imprints her personality on the texts, then stands back, weighing the evidence presented. Sometimes she acts like the narrators of early women's fiction, the novellas of Aphra Behn for example, synthesising public opinion, giving the accepted polite version of a person, then revising it as more is revealed, displaying a concluding but not necessarily final view. John Dashwood enters *Sense and Sensibility* as the 'steady, respectable young man' of common conversation but soon becomes 'not an ill-disposed young man – unless to be rather cold-hearted, and rather selfish, is to be ill-disposed', while Sir John Middleton starts as 'friendly' and his wife 'civil', but soon we hear of the pair's common and 'total want of talent and taste' which makes them hospitable through boredom (*S&S*, 1:7). Sometimes it is unclear whether a statement is comment or free indirect speech, whether it belongs to the narrator or a character; not everything can 'be ascertained' (*NA*, 1:3).

When their common publisher John Murray asked Walter Scott to write a review of *Emma* for the *Quarterly Review* to boost sales, Scott complied with an assessment of Jane Austen as the prime example of a new school of fiction which, eschewing the sensational and melodramatic, sought out the psychologically and socially probable: in this genre 'she stands almost alone'. The praise was high but uneasy – Scott and Austen were writing in different genres and were intellectual and professional if not commercial rivals (*Mansfield Park* sold between 1,000 and 2,000 copies before 1830 where *Guy Mannering* sold 20,000 before 1829). For all his praise Scott, who ignored the achievement of *Mansfield Park*, clearly believed in the greater nationalistic value of his kind of heroic writing, the masculine Romantic style he aptly named the 'Big Bow wow strain'.[16] By contrast, in her defence of the novel in *Northanger Abbey* Austen praises only fiction that conveys 'the most thorough knowledge of human nature'. In 1816 on the last birthday before her death she wrote to her nephew, James Edward Austen-Leigh, who had mislaid some chapters of his never published novel,

> I do not think . . . that any theft of that sort would be really very useful to me. What should I do with your strong, manly, spirited Sketches, full of Variety & Glow? – How could I possibly join them on to the little bit (two Inches wide) of Ivory on which I work with so fine a Brush, as produces little effect after much labour? (*L*, p. 323)

Here the distinction of herself and a writer like Scott is wryly gendered. She is the miniaturist; he the history painter; she paints female domestic spaces, he wide landscapes.

The contrast is not as limiting to Jane Austen as it seems at first. Miniature painting was at its artistic height when she was learning her craft, and her remark is neither an expression of humility nor of artistic insecurity. In *Between Self and World*, James Thompson argues that Austen typically validates emotional depth by using linguistic restraint, suggesting a 'presence beyond the limits of language' by indicating what cannot be directly described.[17] She represents emotion not by the hyperbole of Richardson or Burney but, in her style of restraint, by the odd staccato sentence or fragment of speech. One might extend the artist analogy to the novel heroines. Elinor and in the end Marianne in *Sense and Sensibility* and Fanny in *Mansfield Park* come to accept restraint both as an aesthetic and as an ethic; they live life surrounded by a social frame rather like the miniature's oval one, but, within the confines, are skilled and bold in ways the anarchic or, in novelistic terms, the self-indulgently dramatic, are not.

Our dear, everybody's dear, Jane

Until the late nineteenth century Jane Austen was not widely read, especially compared with her contemporary Walter Scott, her readership being largely confined to some among the titled, gentry, and upper-middle classes and to a few discerning literary people: the early critics Scott and Whately were followed by such appreciative authorities as the philosopher George Henry Lewes and the historian Lord Macaulay. The small but positive initial reception of Austen's work as aesthetically and technically impressive – despite its often remarked 'limitations' – and different from that of other early women writers became one step in the critical uncoupling of the novel from the 'feminine' writing of her sisters: the gothic, sentimental, and didactic authors she enjoyed mocking. As a result, it helped the rise to critical pre-eminence of seemingly ungendered fiction in the nineteenth century.

Much changed in 1870 when James Edward Austen-Leigh published *A Memoir of Jane Austen*, in which he presented his aunt as a modest, ladylike Christian spinster. Together with the novels' portrayal of the last and lost pre-industrial era of England, attractive to a new railway and suburban readership, this work brought a new image to the fore: Austen as national treasure, beloved by 'Janeites'. The image became associated with 'heritage', a smug pastoral Englishness; as the novelist Henry James remarked, the public found 'our dear, everybody's dear, Jane, so infinitely to their material purposes'.

The image annoyed those who associated Jane Austen with class-bound language and subject matter – for D. H. Lawrence she was 'English' 'in the bad, snobbish sense'. The Americans were especially irritated. James Fenimore Cooper claimed he began writing novels because he could certainly do better than Jane Austen; following Walter Scott, he regarded historical romances with sturdy heroes as altogether more masculine than Austen's domestic ones. Ralph Waldo Emerson thought Austen 'vulgar in tone, sterile in artistic invention, imprisoned in the wretched conventions of English society, without genius, wit, or knowledge of the world . . . Suicide is more respectable.' Realising that a ship's library contained no Austen, Mark Twain declared that this 'one omission alone would make a fairly good library out of a library that hadn't a book in it'. For Ezra Pound, Austen presented a 'dull, stupid, hemmed-in sort of life'.[18] To Cooper, Emerson, Twain, Pound, and many other transatlantic male writers she appeared mannered, old-world and claustrophobic, negotiating with, rather than controlling, her environment.

The twentieth century brought a change. Austen gained new intellectual readers and scaled critical heights, famous now for her Augustan irony and technical innovation as well as her delivery of comfort in the Home Counties. The 'dear Jane' of cultural England became by the mid-twentieth century also F. R. Leavis's mother of the morally serious 'Great Tradition' of fiction, the exclusive canon of writers worthy of study in newly established university departments of literature, no longer Henry James's 'homely songbird' but a consummate craftsperson, a laconic satirist and moral teacher. A series of dark critics, especially Reginald Farrer, D. W. Harding, and Marvin Mudrick, proceeded to rescue her from the 'Janeites'. In this bracing atmosphere Ian Watt's influential *The Rise of the Novel* (1957), tracing the 'rise' of formal realism, saw a new modernity in Austen, whose novels achieved an 'authenticity without diffuseness or trickery'.[19]

Feminist criticism of the late 1960s and 1970s saw matters differently. Viewing Jane Austen through the lens of Victorian and modern literature and rebelling against a notion of a masculine-inflected foremother, Sandra Gilbert and Susan Gubar's seminal *The Madwoman in the Attic* (1979) argued that the novels 'explore[d] the tensions between the freedom of her art and the dependency of her characters: while they stutter and sputter and lapse into silence and even hasten to perfect felicity', Austen herself attains a 'woman's language that is magnificently duplicitous'. The proper reader read against the grain, for Austen, like a Victorian woman, was struggling against patriarchy, writing necessarily conservative books which hid within them 'traces of the original duplicity'.[20] Building on this foundation, later versions of feminist criticism saw Austen as symptomatic of the gender conflict of her time: some understood her as voicing not answering questions, others accused her of colluding with patriarchy by advocating heterosexual romance over female relationships.

The focus on Jane Austen as a political writer set in a specific (and distant) past emerged in the 1970s with Alistair Duckworth's *The Improvement of the Estate* (1971) and Marilyn Butler's *Jane Austen and the War of Ideas* (1975), which argued for a writer essentially conservative in religion and politics, composing works which were a fictional embodiment of Edmund Burke's anti-revolutionary manifesto, *Reflections on the Revolution in France* (1790). Burke's hugely influential book celebrated vague visionary ideals of loyalty, chivalry, and organic nationhood, and offered as political model a static society that guarded its inherited hierarchy of constitutional powers and privileges. Key to Burke's philosophy was an unqualified veneration for the past: demanding deference to the British constitution on the grounds of its heritage, *Reflections* contrasted the organic growth of this constitution with the abstract, recent one of revolutionary France. To lend tangible substance to the reverence, Burke made an analogy of the British constitution and the well-run English hereditary estate; *vice versa* he depicted the domestic patriarchal system and the love of 'the little platoon we belong to in society' as the foundation of macrocosmic state order and as 'the germ' of 'public affections'. Burke chided the French National Assembly for overthrowing a defective *ancien régime* constitution: 'you possessed in some parts the walls, and in all the foundations of a noble and venerable castle', he argued. 'Faults of the state' should be approached as 'the wounds of a father', with 'pious awe and trembling solicitude'. Burke's patriarchal ideal of benevolent domination and aristocratic paternalism sought to silence calls for liberal reform; championing the rights of large landowners, *Reflections* mocked notions of a natural and political equality of their tenants – 'How can he get wisdom that holdeth the plough' and 'whose talk is of bullocks?' Soon after the publication of *Reflections*, Burke's rhetoric began to colour political debates and fictional discourse; scores of radical and conservative novelists took up the parallel – associating the head of the state with the head of the household – and used hereditary estates as emblematic reflections of their proprietors' politics and ethics.[21] In the readings of Butler and Duckworth, Jane Austen, while understanding the failures of the upper orders, as Burke himself did, was concerned to shore up the landowning class that ruled and should rule.[22]

Marxist critics, meanwhile, read Austen through a lens of economics, accusing her of endorsing the emergent values of eighteenth-century capitalism and collaborating with the resulting social repression.[23] Crucial here and in most political debates was *Mansfield Park*, seen as a 'state of the nation' work, the equivalent of Scott's *Waverley*, also published in 1814. *Mansfield Park* was central in postcolonial criticism as well, through its mention of slavery. Edward W. Said saw its heroine as a 'trafficked' slave and made her question 'Did not you hear me ask [Sir Thomas] about the slave-trade last night?' followed by 'dead silence!' – crucial to interpretation, for it uncovered the novel's political unconscious: the economic dependency of the grand Mansfield estate on the capitalist exploitation of West Indian slave labour.

Recently, postcolonial, Marxist and feminist approaches have been countered by critical trends that shun ideological perspectives, and a new aestheticism has evolved around analysis of Austen's narrative irony (with D. A. Miller's *Jane Austen, or The Secret of Style*, 2003, probably the most notable study). A resurgence of more traditional scholarship (for example, Roger Gard's *Jane Austen's Novels. The Art of Clarity*, 1992) has been seeking to retrieve her from theory and political interpretation and rescue her for a common readership. Another recent trend in Austen studies is the particular focus on one area of interest alone, such as her reception in a non-European context, her relationship to Romanticism or the Enlightenment, religion, education, the theatre, or food. One significant study, John Wiltshire's *Jane Austen and the Body* (1992), reflects a contemporary interest in the gendered and sexualised body, and its ability to manifest cultural constructions physiologically.

As a result of all this activity, now in the twenty-first century Austen's critical reputation has never stood higher. Her popularity outside the academy of course derives in large part from adaptations, especially of *Pride and Prejudice*: the BBC's 1995 and Hollywood's 2005 versions and the Bollywood-inspired *Bride and Prejudice* of 2004. Everywhere criticism is a lively affair. In book clubs, societies, academic conferences, and university and school classrooms throughout the English-speaking and English-learning world, debates rage about whether we should read with and within as well as against the grain and allow the novels to estrange as well as confirm our own views. Just as divided are attitudes to the heroines: whether they should be regarded as priggish or reeking of sex, and whether they are homoerotic, masturbate, and lack knickers or whether they represent decent, decorous models for our degenerate times.[24]

Chapter 3

Northanger Abbey

Northanger Abbey is about the seduction of the reader, fictional and real. Since reading may control mental construction and perception, it is the comedy of fiction enriching and deforming the life of a single girl.[1] Samuel Johnson claimed that, in the modern romance or 'familiar history', 'the power of example, is so great, as to take possession of the memory by a kind of violence, and produce effects almost without the intervention of the will'.[2] The external reader is caught up in the process, for he or she cannot help believing in the novel's events even as the narrator proclaims them fictional. The mind in and outside the novel is inhabited by stories, including the stories implied by habitual language: the only defence against their control is constant scrutiny, not only of works but of the memory into which they have been transmuted. Using the vehicle of a naïve heroine, *Northanger Abbey* studies the creation of subjectivity through language and its images. Since it is also a novel with a novel's plot, it delivers a satisfactory story in which a sophisticated hero is seduced by sparkling eyes and girlish adoration.

Northanger Abbey had the longest gestation of any Austen work: published posthumously in 1818, it was first drafted in 1798–9, revised in 1803 and prepared for publication in 1816, so inhabiting three historical moments.[3] Austen was keen to locate the novel in its main material time of the 1790s and 1803 rather than 1816; to this end she provided an 'advertisement' by the 'Authoress', pointing out the quotidian nature of its details:

> some observation is necessary upon those parts of the work which thirteen years have made comparatively obsolete. The public are entreated to bear in mind that thirteen years have passed since it was finished, many more since it was begun, and that during that period, places, manners, books, and opinions have undergone considerable changes.

She knew that fashions and hairstyles had altered and that the muslins in style in 1803 differed from the fabrics wanted in 1816. She also knew that people were reading different books and that, in terms of psychology and mind–body relation, character was perceived differently. Also, she herself had changed: the light-hearted tone about politics and work in *Northanger Abbey* suggests the young Steventon woman rather than the Chawton professional.

I have Udolpho to read

The plot of *Northanger Abbey* concerns a young girl, Catherine, with the dullest home life of any Austen heroine. One summer she leaves her village with friends for Bath where she is introduced to society and love. For the latter she has an easy choice between the vulgar and boorishly masculine John Thorpe and the skittish, gentlemanly, more androgynous Henry Tilney, although her liking for her new friend, John's sister Isabella, gives her some distrust of her initial instincts, and there are never quite admitted resemblances between the two overbearing suitors. Having at home read mainly in improving literature and poetic extracts, her starved imagination is overwhelmed by the power of gothic fiction when she encounters Mrs Radcliffe's world of sensational events, mysterious castles, orphaned heroines, and commanding villains.

Others in her circle are equally in thrall to 'fictions', but within real life: under the influence of Thorpe's selfish exaggeration, Henry's father, the imposing general, comes to believe Catherine an heiress; so he invites her to his abbey to secure her for his son. There, her head full of gothic expectations, she begins to make her own fiction, transforming the modernised house into the site of wife-murder and its selfish owner into a literary villain, until ejected by him when her wealth proves illusory. By now she has recovered from her gothic fears, and, although the kindly daughter Eleanor melodramatically refers to her as 'driven out of the house', she faces with equanimity a potentially unpleasant journey home alone. There Catherine encounters her old image as a 'sad little shatter-brained creature' – a diminution the gothic orphan never faces – until elevated to heroine status by the arrival of Henry. The pair achieve 'perfect happiness at the respective ages of twenty-six and eighteen'. Romance and realism come together in mutual affectionate mockery.

Conduct books and didactic novels indicated the crucial importance of reading in the formation of a girl's mind and almost everyone saw danger in a promiscuous consumption of imaginative fiction, especially with the new consumerist reading habits which encouraged rapidity rather than depth of response. The main fear was sexual and social. That adult men were consuming pornography provoked less cultural anxiety than the notion of the young middle-class virgin learning from romance to expect more from life than she was likely to get. The anxiety, in some form as old as printed fiction, intensified markedly with the growth of domestic romances aimed directly at women. A typical warning voice was that of the conduct-book writer and clergyman James Fordyce, admired by the ridiculous Mr Collins in *Pride and Prejudice*. Fordyce writes of 'swarms of foolish and of worthless novels, incessantly spawned by dull and by dissolute scribblers, and with unwearied industry disseminated from our Circulating Libraries', destroying 'virtuous principle' and introducing 'impure ideas, extravagant desires, and notions of happiness alike fantastic and false'.[4]

The poet and philosopher Samuel Taylor Coleridge asked of the gothic novel, 'Can these things be admired without a bad effect on the mind – '.[5] The answer from Henry Tilney, and in the end Catherine, was of course 'yes' if read with care. Like Tilney and most literate men and women of the time, Austen herself was steeped in Radcliffe's work and, while there is much burlesque in *Northanger Abbey*, especially of *The Romance of the Forest*, which provides creepy parallels to the abbey imaginings, and *The Mysteries of Udolpho*, which engrosses Catherine in Bath, both are appreciated for their powerful engagement of the reader with their terrified but resourceful heroines. In relation to these young women modern criticism has made much of the gothic's depiction of sexual fear through its creation of frightening spaces and winding passages, and indeed for Catherine the appeal of the gothic comes when she has been sexually aroused by Henry in Bath. Yet she clearly responds to the gothic's *literary* appeal. Desire to know a story overwhelms incipient erotic feelings: 'while I have Udolpho to read, I feel as if nobody could make me miserable', she remarks – a nice comment on the conduct-book anxieties that saw fiction enflaming the girl's sexual desire. (Other aspects of Mrs Radcliffe's achievement pass Catherine by: she would not have needed so much aesthetic instructing had she read the picturesque passages of *Udolpho* with more care.)

For Catherine, the fictional *Udolpho* becomes something close to true experience and memory, as she reveals when, contemplating English rain, she sighs for weather from the south of France. Ridiculed out of direct application of fiction to modern England, she yet holds on to what she has grasped: that real-life men may resemble gothic villains without murdering their wives and that, in and out of novels, people are motivated by greed. With her refreshingly small amount of self-obsession, she once had a susceptible but undeveloped imagination, the result of life with an unimaginative family – her mother even fails to think of lovers or romance when her teenage daughter leaves home – and only reading jolts her out of her easy acceptance of authenticity in everyone. In the end, fiction helps her not only to enrich her memory but also to understand that people have a 'general though unequal mixture of good and bad'.

Is there a Henry . . .?

Henry Tilney's high spirits delight Catherine and his gentle mocking of her delights him with his own superiority, so they are well pleased with each other. He enlivens the trivia of conventional conversation with an ebullient misogyny and knowingness, introducing her to tropes and genres outside the reach of her commonsensical family – satire, irony, simile and metaphor, all as new to Catherine as the sensational fiction of Mrs Radcliffe. In the first few encounters she learns that language must be scrutinised since it is not transparent. When she perceives Mrs Allen's pleasure in Henry's mimicked conversation she begins to see how people might be manipulated by speech. Henry also instructs her in the ulterior uses of talk for flirtation, suggesting how the refusal to answer an intentionally forward or impolite question can lead to intimacy. By the time she is actually complimented by him as having a mind 'warped by an innate principle of general integrity', Catherine's unsentimental education has gone so far that she has an inkling of irony. In due course Henry's encouragement draws out what is in Catherine rather than imposing a system from without. When they have been in the abbey for some time she receives her brother's letter revealing Isabella's desertion; Henry prompts Catherine to express conventional sentimental anguish over her friend's duplicity and waits for her to achieve the correct judicious response. When Catherine replies as he wishes, he advises and compliments: 'Such feeling ought to be investigated, that they may know themselves.'

All overt instruction holds the potential for both bullying and erotically arousing, and the mentor Henry is not presented as the ultimate authority in the book. Some of his remarks are themselves ironised and suggest self-ironising, as when he muses that women's abilities are 'neither sound nor acute'. There is a bit of the Bath 'quiz' about his enjoyment of female discomfiture as well as of the harassing type Thorpe represents more fully, and he can be pedantic, overconcerned to create his version of order. He mocks Catherine's imprecise and affected language, her overuse of 'nice'. Samuel Johnson strove for an ideal of grammatical purity and 'laboured' to rid English of 'colloquial barbarisms, licentious idioms, and irregular combinations'; here Henry objects to the corruption of a precise word under the influence of the vulgar and modish, his criticism recalling Jane Austen's own linguistic stringency, her habit of fixing foolish characters through the imprecision of their language.[6] Yet, despite not fitting the definitions of a generation back found in Johnson's *Dictionary* (1755), which supports only Henry's senses of accurate, neat, and precise, Catherine's use has the modern meaning of 'pleasant' and is acceptable in conversation, if speaker and listener agree; the narrator's mild irony envelops both the careless user and the purist who tries to arrest the fluidity of language.

Although his verbal skills far surpass Catherine's, some of her naïve comments have a clarity Henry seldom achieves. When she remarks at cross purposes to Henry's sophisticated meaning, 'I cannot speak well enough to be unintelligible', he regards it as simply a comic comment on modern linguistic habits, where the reader may see her drawing attention to the obfuscating uses of language, including his own. Henry mocks the repeated clichés of ordinary conversation, but these are primarily a matter of social stroking, and his sister usefully employs them 'with simplicity and truth, and without personal conceit'.

Sometimes Catherine is silenced before she should be, not only by Henry's bullying pedagogy but also by his unexpected restraint. Misjudging the general – to whom his children rarely speak honestly – as well as his eldest son, she urges Henry to intervene in Captain Tilney's flirtation with Isabella. Henry stops the conversation – rather as his father will later do when he meets anything distasteful. He knows the outcome but will not enlighten Catherine and help her dim-witted brother James, and she sees what Henry never admits, that his brother is as blameworthy as Isabella. Earlier, when he mocks the confusion of his sister and Catherine over something 'uncommonly dreadful' coming out of London – the fiction-obsessed Catherine thinks of gothic fiction and the history-reading Eleanor assumes riots – Henry fails to make a reasonable connection between societal upheavals and fictional excess in their use of the language of horror. A similar effect occurs when he lists among the virtues of middle England the 'neighbourhood of voluntary spies', possibly referring both to nosy neighbours and to agents of the Pitt government used to inform on radicals and subversives during the early war years. The latter are part of the same turbulent national culture that produced the patriotic gothic novel of the 1790s, with its frightening picture of Catholic Europe and its 'pines and vices'. When Henry reprimands Catherine for her suspicions about his parents, forcing her to take her belief in a Radcliffean realm beyond English shores, he properly points to the cultural distinction of England with its advanced social and legal system which protects wives against murder. But he fails to anticipate Catherine's later perception that there is something radically wrong with the English general. If she has been mistaken in judging through Radcliffe's Italian villains that Henry's father is a wife-murderer, Henry is not entirely right to mock her: by the end he apparently comes to agree with her that the general has been cruel in his very English pursuit of money.

Some irony also touches Henry when he teaches picturesque taste, a subject discussed in the late eighteenth and early nineteenth centuries by William

Gilpin, Uvedale Price, and Richard Payne Knight, along with the landscape gardener Humphrey Repton, heir and critic of 'Capability' Brown. Now that we do not aestheticise nature in the way we do cultural artefacts, it is hard to capture the heatedness of a debate in which the contested word 'picturesque' was variously used but rarely defined – perhaps necessarily since it became more than an artistic term, affecting general ways of seeing and perceiving. In its more specific use, it denoted 'that peculiar kind of beauty which is agreeable in a picture', the kind that lent itself to being represented or sketched by a human observer.[7] Scenes should be apprehended in foreground, middle distance, and background, with light, shade, and texture helping to form a single expressive and affective whole. Here the main theorist was William Gilpin, and Henry Austen noted that 'at a very early age' his sister was 'enamoured of Gilpin on the Picturesque' (*Memoir*, pp. 140–1); this must have been a bookish enthusiasm since her nephew James Edward Austen-Leigh insisted on the unpicturesque nature of the Steventon landscape (*Memoir*, p. 21). In *Observations, Relative chiefly to Picturesque Beauty* (1786) Gilpin provides 'a sort of analytic view of the materials which compose [picturesque scenes] – *mountains – lakes . . . rocks – cascades – vallies –* and *rivers*'.[8]

Earlier in the century there had been discussion about whether taste was based on universal innate principles or had to be taught: picturesque theory assumed the latter. Although Henry Tilney in gallant mode declares Catherine has 'natural taste', the picturesque was a learnt method of reading and creating a scene so that it interacted with aesthetic expectations – Henry 'places' a rocky fragment and 'withered oak' near the summit of his viewed landscape. Following Gilpin, the Tilneys do have 'real taste' but Austen retreats from absolutes; as Gilpin himself knew, any method could be taken to extremes, as it is when Henry first excludes Catherine from the conversation on Beechen Cliff and then imposes rules which prevent her delighting in the view of Bath or when, in opposition to the social urgings of Richard Payne Knight and the later Repton, the general would move a cottage simply to improve a casual view.[9]

As with other philosophies and theories, Jane Austen enjoys less explicating than humorously using picturesque ideas. Henry delivers them in flirtatious mode and moves from a discussion to silence, broken only when Catherine mentions the gothic novel. Although hidden from his sister Eleanor, the train of thought from the picturesque to the gothic (both imaginative ways of seeing) makes sense to Catherine and Henry, and the agreement, although Henry uses it to laugh at women, brings them coyly together. Shared viewing, like shared reading, can be a pleasurable exchange. Catherine feels its erotic aspect and learns quickly because she is already in love.

Seduction, the narrator suggests, is 'administering to the vanity of others'. This is a theme Austen will develop throughout her works, culminating in the eloquent seduction by Anne Elliot in the final novel, *Persuasion*. Catherine attracts the clever Henry with her naïvety and obvious admiration. When he tries to stand on dignity after her social *faux pas* of reneging on the promised walk, she simply declares she would have jumped from the carriage to run after him if she could: 'is there a Henry in the world who could be insensible to such a declaration?' asks the narrator.

Only a novel

In a novel so much about novels it is appropriate that many characters are fictionists themselves, eager to manipulate real people into their scenes and plots, but not as honest about their acts as the narrator. Since she is at this point constructing herself in the mode of fashionable sentiment, Isabella is immediate bosom friends with Catherine – in the manner of the intuitive heroines of sentimental novels – although she is in fact no great reader and uses books only as tools of flirtation. Wearing this sentimental mask, she gives Catherine an equally intuitive and shallow character; when Catherine is supposed to have discerned tenderness between her friend and her brother, Isabella declares: 'You would have told us that we seemed born for each other, or some nonsense of that kind, which would have distressed me beyond conception; my cheeks would have been as red as your roses' (*NA*, 1:10). Catherine rejects the remark as foreign to her character: having an inkling of the erotic understanding into which she is being propelled, she terms the imputed sentiment 'improper'.

Later, when Isabella remodels herself as pert woman of the world for the more sophisticated Captain Tilney, she revises her language and reinvents the engagement with James as a little harmless flirtation, commenting, 'what one means one day, you know, one may not mean the next' (here she attacks the old-fashioned and honourable code of promises, made or implied, which will keep Henry true to Catherine in the face of his father's opposition but which will be ignored in the opening of *Sense and Sensibility*). In this new character she has to remake her friend, telling her not to be so 'abominably affected'. Catherine should aim at 'a little common honesty' – for show, of course, since it is more 'becoming'. The chameleon character bewilders Catherine. When she receives Isabella's wheedling letter, she is both enlightened about her friend and about the layering of language: 'Its inconsistencies, contradictions, and falsehood struck her from the very first' (*NA*, 2:12). Genteelly poor Isabella, unskilfully playing the marriage market, is allowed no sympathy from Catherine or Henry.

A man's world has larger compass. Where both John and Isabella Thorpe tell lies to 'increase their importance', John's more easily affect the social context. In the space of the book he rattles through London, Oxford, and Bath, as a result imposing his fictions twice on General Tilney, making Catherine first a great heiress, then a pauper. With Catherine he is less insinuating and he quickly bores her by his invented dialogues. So outrageous does he become that she rebukes him: 'If I could not be persuaded into doing what I thought wrong, I never will be tricked into it' (*NA*, 1:13).

Henry's fictions are as controlling as the Thorpes', but Catherine is a more willing auditor, and her admiration spurs him on. His stories reach their apogee on the ride to the abbey where, working with the plots Radcliffe has impressed on Catherine, he makes the journey a voyage into the gothic, transforming ordinary domestic items into uncanny props of suspense. Amused by his success, he breaks off before Radcliffean closure, leaving Catherine without narrative guide when she enters his house. Alone she gothicises the two props Henry omitted from his story, the general and his daughter, seeing in the former the lineaments of the villain and in the latter those of the melancholy, oppressed heroine.

Henry is aghast at her temerity – although to herself she blames *him* for the leap she has made – and his usual chastising eloquence falters: 'If I understand you rightly, you had formed a surmise of such horror as I have hardly words to –' (*NA*, 2:9). When at the end of the novel he himself has to confront his father's social villainy, he is again suitably wordless. The tables turn and the reader learns that, where Catherine has had an education mainly in transparency from her family, Henry has been schooled in repression and hypocrisy, having watched his father say one thing and mean another and having learned constantly to curb his own speech. Hence perhaps his attraction to the spontaneous Catherine: the 'gratitude' that makes him love her includes appreciation of her freedom from all that has made his home life so stultifying.

A second reading of the novel makes Henry's figurative use of language seem less playful, more of a defence against the impossibility of truth-telling. It also clarifies his occasional ambiguous reticence: both he and his sister act at their father's behest in inviting Catherine to dinner and then to the abbey, knowing that the general must have some scheme afoot. It becomes apparent how much memory of home life permeates Henry's mind, how much his role-playing has been a necessary defence rather than social play or bid for power. Until the end, through filial fear and respect and perhaps the need for continuing patronage and largesse, Henry has not stood up to his father either for himself, for his friend Catherine, or for his uncomfortably placed sister.

Paradoxically, he comes closest to Catherine's gothic literary heroes after he finally allows some gothic aspects to his father. Always aware of the general's selfish oppression, at last he dares 'to clothe' his 'opposing desire' 'in words'. Then, to Catherine's literary delight, he becomes the man who defies his father for love – happily her old pre-gothic self is appeased by his proposing to her *before* telling her of the paternal opposition, so avoiding her need to indulge in 'conscientious rejection'. The *éclaircissement* removes Catherine further from the general's clutches: formerly given 'elasticity of walk' by him, when she learns the reason for his admiration and its removal, she 'hardened' into delight at their reversal of power.

Beyond the Thorpes and Henry Tilney, there is in *Northanger Abbey* the controlling fictionist, the narrator herself, who moves in and out of Catherine's mind using direct comment and free indirect speech. In the later books there will be a sophisticated use of fractured, emotive language: here the use of breathless syntax is mainly parodic, recalling Radcliffe's own creation of her anxious heroines. When Catherine arrives at the abbey and learns of the death of the general's wife, the narrator employs Catherine's newly acquired language of gothic writing for the response: 'her blood ran cold with the horrid suggestions . . . What could more plainly speak the gloomy workings of a mind not wholly dead to every sense of humanity, in its fearful review of past scenes of guilt? Unhappy man!' (*NA*, 2:8). As Catherine moves from gothic influence, the narrator uses a less mocking tone for her inner processes: when she starts to see the selfishness of Isabella, 'these painful ideas crossed her mind'. Pain is present in *Northanger Abbey* in James Morland's jilting and Eleanor's melancholy youth, but, unlike in *Persuasion*, with which it was published and which in Anne Elliot echoes Eleanor's story, there is usually irony. The narrator is most frequently complicit with us as readers, for we would not have expected Northanger to be gothic and would have suspected Isabella's sincerity rather earlier than Catherine. On these occasions the heroine functions as a comic reprise of the female 'quixote', whose mind is addled by romantic fiction. The chief of these is Charlotte Lennox's Arabella in *The Female Quixote* (1752), who, through various adventures, comes thuddingly to right thinking (the work 'now makes our evening amusement', Austen wrote of Lennox's novel in 1807, *L*, p. 116). In *Northanger Abbey*, as in *The Female Quixote*, the narrator insists by analogy that we do not immerse ourselves simply in the fictional world, but remain aware of a metafictional level demanding analytic response.

Throughout *Northanger Abbey* there are references to the reader reading this and other books, references which curb the desire to identify with characters and experience suspense. Towards the end, when we have been allowed to feel for Catherine in her painful ejection from the abbey, the narrator cuts through this empathy by reinvoking the gothic, making her sad and indecorous return home into sensational 'solitude and disgrace'. The same insistent instability occurs at the close when Eleanor's true unsettling situation is described. Knowing that her 'real power is nothing', she has been the patient, long-suffering daughter dependent on a selfish father; now she is rescued by a fairy-tale viscount, welded on to the plot to fulfil romance and mock the novel. The burlesque element remains – the novelist enjoys wrapping up the work as arbitrarily as the picturesque viewer inserts a withered oak into the scene on view, and both Catherine and Eleanor benefit.

Like Sterne in *Tristram Shandy*, the narrator creates different fictional readers in this text – what Gerald Prince calls 'narratees': she assumes sometimes an astute novel reader with knowledge of fictional conventions and at others 'every young lady', who is only now experiencing what Catherine experiences.[10] She also creates different novelists, for example when she follows, then mocks, the habit of didactic digression. Having provided a discourse on clothes, which, in its concern for social effect rather than principle, is of dubious morality, she comments: 'But not one of these grave reflections troubled the tranquillity of Catherine' (*NA*, 1:10). Here and elsewhere, the narrator creates expectations in the reader, then disrupts them by ridicule or fulfils them indulgently as with the closing fairy-tale 'felicity'. When she comments on the attraction of ignorance in pretty girls, we may be made uneasy, feeling some bitterness about the female predicament; then she provides the more comforting notion that not everyone wants 'imbecility in females'. The effect is then undercut by the remark that 'reasonable and well-informed men only want ignorance'. With such techniques, readers are encouraged to interpret and respond critically to all fiction and fiction-makers.

Henry Tilney calls the denigrator of 'a good novel' 'intolerably stupid' – presumably using the extreme adverb intentionally. And the assertive narrator, expressing perhaps Jane Austen's resentment at the rejection of 'First Impressions', provides a comically serious defence of the form beginning with an imagined encounter with an insecure reader – '"what are you reading, Miss?" "Oh! It is only a novel!"' – and condemning such deprecation as 'common cant'. In this defence, instead of praising the male tradition of Henry Fielding and Samuel Richardson, the narrator elevates Frances Burney and Maria Edgeworth as supreme novelists. Yet, as usual in Austen, nothing is quite what it seems at first. She knows that Burney and Edgeworth are writing novels for entertainment, as she is; so there is some irony in the allusion here to their own stance. In the second preface to *Evelina*, Burney had praised only male writers and wished for 'the total extirpation of novels' that infect 'our young ladies in general, and boarding-school damsels in particular' with 'distemper'; Edgeworth's 'Advertisement' to *Belinda* claims 'The following work is offered to the public as a Moral Tale – the author not wishing to acknowledge a Novel.'[11]

Chapter 4

Sense and Sensibility

To excite or moderate passions

The picture of Isabella in *Northanger Abbey* portrayed sensibility as a cultural fad that allowed manipulative and morally trivial people to appropriate a rhetoric of feeling so as to further their own selfish schemes. But in *Sense and Sensibility*, a novel conceived earlier, Austen chose as one of two heroines a genuine young woman whose inner thought processes and perceptions of the exterior world were thoroughly permeated and shaped by sentimental language and its moral values.

As a result of its long gestation, when published in 1811, *Sense and Sensibility* struck novel-readers as displaying a 'want of *newness*'.[1] It seemed to belong to its moment of conception rather than to its time of publication during the Regency. Echoing such schematic works as Elizabeth Inchbald's *Nature and Art* (1796), its title of contrasting abstractions evoked the anxious dualities of the 1790s, reason and feeling, liberty and slavery, revolution and restraint. Its two heroines recalled pairs of contrasting girls from the period, in Inchbald's *A Simple Story* (1791) and Jane West's *A Gossip's Story* (1796), the latter opposing the lovely, romantic, and indulged Marianne to the sensible and reserved Louisa. The revisions that transformed the epistolary 'Elinor and Marianne' into the third-person *Sense and Sensibility* were no doubt considerable but apparently had not tampered with the basic structure. As a result, the novel feels politically conservative in the polarised terms of the 1790s: providing a cure for romantic excess and mocking the emotional spontaneity which to many appeared the essence of sensibility, source both of French revolutionary intemperance and of failing British fortitude.

Yet the appearance is deceptive and, with careful or repeated reading, *Sense and Sensibility* belies its crude, schematic appearance, collapsing the easy antithesis of self-control and emotionalism. Instead of simply contrasting Elinor and Marianne, it works with the structural possibilities of two heroines to investigate how a person can live in the world without giving it too much and without growing alienated by its demands and indifference. The book becomes one of Austen's bleakest visions of society, as well as a disturbing portrait of the destructive power of sexual love to consume and isolate. I have claimed that Austen's works converse with each other and can be interpreted through these conversations. One of the least favourite among readers, *Sense and Sensibility* is in dialogue with one of the most favoured, *Persuasion*, on the value of heterosexual love – not illicit sexual activity, the subject of more polemical books of the time, but romantic passion. In both novels, passion is investigated as the powerful irrational force David Hume exposed: 'To diminish . . . or augment any person's value . . . to excite or moderate his passions, there are no direct arguments or reasons, which can be employed with any force or influence.'[2] Passion is also studied as a cultural force in which literature and art are intimately implicated.

In keeping with its dual title, *Sense and Sensibility* tells echoing stories of two of three sisters, Elinor and the younger Marianne Dashwood, the latter sixteen at the beginning of the book, all ejected in relative poverty from their father's house through the will of their great-uncle, who leaves much of his fortune to their half-brother and his three-year-old son. As the Austen women were rescued and given lodgings by Edward Knight, the Dashwoods are provided with Barton Cottage by Sir John Middleton, a distant relative. Both sisters fall in love, one publicly and noisily, the other more quietly and privately but, it appears later, with similar intensity. Both love before they have social licence to do so, although both feel sure in their hearts that their love is returned.

Their beloved men are Edward Ferrars, Elinor's diffident, good-hearted and secretly engaged brother-in-law, and Marianne's charming and worldly Willoughby. Where Henry Tilney was mundanely presented to Catherine on the dance floor, Willoughby is introduced through a chivalric rescue of Marianne, who has tumbled down a hill in wild weather. By all the Dashwood women he is declared everything a young man should be, with his glamorous hunting dress, dogs and horses, a fairy-tale prince in a pastoral scene. When, as the plot unfolds, the sisters appear to be losing their suitors, Marianne acts with abandon, Elinor with cunning and control. As a result, Marianne follows the sentimental trajectory of the abandoned maid by sickening and almost dying, until rescued by a combination of her own good sense and loving family, while Elinor, constrained by social awareness, creates for herself a carapace which prevents family pity and public exposure. In the end Elinor achieves her first love, not through deserving him but through the selfishness of her rival – and only after suffering the theatrical error of believing him already married. Under family pressure, Marianne settles for the earlier despised Colonel Brandon and a comfortable manor house. Sentiment and prudence, or sense, emotion, and reason, are not separate but function as abstractions allowing people to generalise and judge. Society and the individual are always partly antagonistic and partly nurturing, while passion and desire, if not to be destructive, must negotiate with self-protection. The book certainly differs from a 1790s conduct book advising a person to act like 'sensible' Elinor, but it may become a guide on how to cope with a harsh society, using sometimes Marianne's habitual method of wishful projection, sometimes Elinor's empirical scrutiny, and often the narrator's wry humour.

Having set up her dualistic title and two heroines, Austen revels in duplicating and shadowing. The vulgar Lucy and Anne Steele, who cause Elinor such pain, echo the more refined Dashwoods in their poverty and need to marry – Lucy and Elinor are dishonest with each other and both play parts – while the daughters of the garrulous, kind-hearted Mrs Jennings repeat in cruder form the contrast of Elinor and Marianne. The mothers too come together, since Mrs Dashwood and Mrs Jennings each love best one of their daughters for her resemblance to herself. Colonel Brandon's dead beloved and her daughter, now his ward, both called Eliza and relegated through their scandalous acts to an inserted tale, duplicate each other and Marianne in suffering. Even more insistently, the men seem interchangeable. One will be confidently expected by Elinor, only for another to walk in. Marianne stares at an approaching rider, sure it is Willoughby, but finds Edward materialising. In London, when Willoughby is passionately wanted, the visitor is most often Colonel Brandon. The men are jealous of each other; having wronged Marianne *and* Colonel Brandon through his seduction of the second Eliza, Willoughby worries that the pair might marry, while Edward, having secretly engaged himself to Lucy Steele, fears that Elinor will have the colonel. Meanwhile, the colonel is consumed with jealousy for the seducing Willoughby. The repeated substitutions make men appear an alien species to the women who wait for them, flitting about with little forewarning of their exits and entrances.

This is quite another thing

More than any other Austen novel, *Sense and Sensibility* fulfils Auden's comic quip about the 'amorous effects of "brass"', for money is a constant topic of rich and poor. People ponder how much they owe and are owed, and the book hums with precise sums. Like *Clarissa*, Richardson's great novel of family cruelty, it begins with a will, providing a dark satire on family property arrangements, especially for women. (But no easy feminist point is made: if primogeniture and entail favour men, money in the power of women with no legal constraints leads to abuse.) Owing to this will, a mixture of customary primogeniture and arbitrary carelessness, the Dashwood sisters fall from the ranks of the landed gentry, living on a country estate yielding £4,000 a year, to becoming recipients of an annual £500, inhabiting a charitably rented cottage.

Blessed with several fortunes, their half-brother John Dashwood sees everything in monetary terms – suggesting that extremes of prudential 'sense' are more socially dangerous than the self-destructive extremes of 'sensibility'. In the masterly conversation he has with his wife Fanny at the beginning of the novel, reminiscent of the dialogue of the wicked sisters with their father in *King Lear*, the deathbed promise to his father of considerable help, initially construed as £3,000, is whittled down to the occasional present; it ends with Fanny picturing the life of unmarried ladies once their male provider is dead: without carriage or horses, with hardly any servants and no company, 'how comfortable they will be'. Putting aside a verbal promise, the imaginative Fanny makes a convincing scenario of patriarchal prudential concern for the single male heir, 'poor little Harry', that overwhelms her weaker husband. In the shoddy world of legal formalities she reformulates the 'independence' which should carry with it not only an implication of gentility but also the social and financial care of dependants – relatives and those less well-off – into its opposite: living without care for anyone outside the nuclear family. In this instance, language impinges directly on conduct.

Yet it is rarely a simple matter of the authentic versus the inauthentic. Many of the conversations between Elinor and Marianne turn on how much it is one's duty to 'tell lies when politeness requires it' – Austen does not flinch from using this word to denote the social trivia Marianne so hates – and at what point hypocrisy becomes downright duplicity. The spontaneity and self-centred energy of Willoughby and Marianne is attractive – before we learn that Willoughby, in Mr Knightley's words for Mr Elton in *Emma*, talks 'sentimentally, but . . . will act rationally'. The pair attract when they mock their crude acquaintances and express the contempt Elinor represses, but not when they ridicule the benevolent Colonel Brandon. Elinor argues the need for self-respect and pride to curb the tongue and employ subtlety and secrecy. This stance helps smooth social relations and avoids exposing the self to rudeness and raillery. By contrast, Marianne allows one emotion to grow so large in herself and her world that it empties her of others, obliterating all outside; as a result she sometimes seems almost autistic in her refusal to connect or contrive. Initially she despises subterfuge, but she finds she cannot endure the pity to which openness exposes her; cunning Lucy Steele never loses self-respect – when Edward fails to contact her, she suspects delinquency but refrains from importuning him as Marianne does Willoughby: 'her spirit rose against' writing.

The unpleasant, vacuous society that makes up so much of *Sense and Sensibility* is tolerable mainly through the operation of the cold quality of civility with its conventional circulating words. Austen portrays exchanges made bearable only by social phrases and learned decorum. Suffering from kindly stupidity, Elinor sometimes finds herself rating 'good breeding as more indispensable to comfort than good nature'. The book suggests a harsh determinism by which some characters cannot be reformed, but civility can be acquired even by the thoroughly nasty. Selfish Fanny Dashwood treats her in-laws 'with quiet civility' during a stay of six months, and the empty Lady Middleton saves the Dashwood sisters from her well-meaning but irritating mother's raillery through remarks on the weather. Never using it for social stroking, Marianne only notices the weather in moments of heightened emotion and almost always misjudges it. The codes of civility protect and constrain, but one can expect too much from them. Mrs Dashwood assumes that all their friends will drop Willoughby once he has exposed his villainy, but Lady Middleton resolves at once to call on his new wife as 'a woman of elegance and fortune'.

The use and abuse of civility are well exemplified in the climactic ball, where Willoughby snubs Marianne, who exclaims and cries out after him. Elinor tries to screen her sister from exposing her hurt to the public gaze, while Willoughby hides behind the social forms of the ballroom, so wittily mocked by Henry Tilney. Lady Middleton is playing cards but her adherence to civil codes means that, while not caring in the least for Marianne, she is 'too polite to object for a moment' and drives her home when requested. 'There is a quintessential truth about the conditions of life in society expressed in that quiet struggle between screaming and screening.'[3]

Lady Middleton's useful but hackneyed language of civility is matched by her employment of words 'in common use', like 'satirical' as a form of abuse, without knowing their meaning. Margaret, the dullest and youngest of the Dashwood sisters, along with Anne Steele, uses most 'novel slang' – 'Marianne's preserver' for Willoughby for example. At the other extreme, Marianne declares she is sometimes silent to avoid speaking falsely or in jargon. Instead of a common language, she wants something close to an idiolect. Down-to-earth Edward Ferrars mocks her linguistic anxiety by imagining her wishing to burn her poetry books to prevent their words being read by the dull and conventional. In his last intrusion into the Dashwoods' lives, the flexible Willoughby reveals that he seduced Marianne by mimicking her language. He – and their romance – has been Marianne's creation, not his. When he betrays her, he employs his fiancée's words in his letter. In the end, in the conversation with Elinor he is left with nothing except clichés to describe what he believes to be intense feeling. By contrast, Austen triumphs, for her restrained technique has allowed one suppressed scream to carry more anguish than the feverish hysterics and hyperbolic language of countless disappointed or abandoned women in contemporary novels.

Words and things intermingle. The narrator shadows ordinary Barton Cottage with a picturesque image: it is 'defective . . . for the building was regular, the roof was tiled, the window shutters were not painted green, nor were the walls covered with honeysuckles'. The place becomes a vehicle for Willoughby's seductive sentimentality when he insists it must be preserved in aspic, while Mrs Dashwood's overambitious plans on a small income are topped by Robert Ferrars's vision of a cottage with library, saloon, and dining room for eighteen couples. Smaller items assume idiosyncratic significance. For the mean Fanny Dashwood, the grand family china gives improper distinction to the new low status of her in-laws, while an insolently contemplated toothpick case declares to Elinor the solipsistic vacuity of Fanny's foppish brother Robert Ferrars.

David Hume declared that objects were valueless unless invested with value by human passions. This is true of the personal objects which change according to their perceivers. The hair in Edward's ring dupes Elinor into hope when she assumes it her own. Her assumption sits oddly with her disapproval of Marianne's voluntarily giving a lock to Willoughby. Here Elinor appears quite as able as Marianne to gull herself, despite knowing the decorum of such intimate bodily gifts. In the end, the hair both Edward and Willoughby receive is not treasured. Miniature portraits and letters also circulate and alter in emotional significance. Marianne, it appears, has recently worn a miniature round her neck which, after much speculation from her sisters, turns out to be of her great-uncle – who has left them very little. The usual reason why a person would wear a miniature of an old relative is in hope of inheriting or in gratitude for having done so; the detail suggests Marianne's refusal to enter the system of money relationships in which her worldly lover Willoughby is enmeshed. Elinor, her cannier sister, knows this use of personal items: when faced with Willoughby's owning such a miniature she immediately construes it may belong to 'some great uncle of *his*'. But she is not always canny about the meaning of portraits. When Lucy Steele takes a 'small miniature from her pocket' to give her rival material proof of her engagement, Elinor has no doubts of 'its being Edward's face' but tries to transform it into a sign of waning love. It guards its meaning, however, since neither woman knows what its possession now signifies. All these objects are, as Hume described, invested with value by human passion and they change according to the emotional environment. People try to control their meaning but are no more successful than Henry Tilney when, in *Northanger Abbey*, he tried to stabilise the meaning of words.

Delicacy of passion

With its emphasis on responsive feeling, sensibility could promote self-absorption. As Hume wrote: 'Some people are subject to a certain *delicacy of passion*, which makes them extremely sensible to all the accidents of life, and gives them a lively joy upon every prosperous event, as well as a piercing grief, when they meet with misfortunes and adversity . . . men of such lively passions are apt to be transported beyond all bounds of prudence and discretion, and to take false steps in the conduct of life, which are often irretrievable.'[4] Having little truck with internal or external guards, sensibility seemed to conduct-book writers easily eroticised and Fordyce, in particular, urged girls to be restrained so as to defend themselves against seduction. Marianne delights in abandoned driving and illicit visiting, and she insists that intuitive morality needs no investigation: 'if there had been any real impropriety in what I did, I should have been sensible of it at the time, for we always know when we are acting wrong'. Elinor disagrees that pleasure equals rectitude. Although the feeling Marianne espouses is instinctive, the narrator stresses how much of it is also artificial and formed by repetition and association. Marianne's grief over leaving her home and over Willoughby's absence is 'voluntarily renewed'. The two griefs are consecutive: at first so lamented, home quickly recedes before sexual involvement.

In *Northanger Abbey* the reader regarded young Catherine through the amused eyes of the narrator. Similarly, Marianne is often the victim of sardonic remarks and the result may seem heavy-handed: providing real grief for a 'real' young woman, the narrator mocks it as if both were items in the *Juvenilia*. Marianne is rarely seen from inside; unlike Colonel Brandon with the Elizas, she does not tell her love story coherently but lets it emerge in fragments.[5] Elinor converses, replies, and receives confidences which she then processes, but Marianne can only express what she thinks at the moment or be silent. The free indirect discourse with which Austen is experimenting is not as supple a device as in the later works and, as with the narrative voice, its allowed irony sometimes seems at odds with Marianne's suggested inner life.

Marianne is distanced and filtered through Elinor's mental processes. More than in *Northanger Abbey* we are allowed into this heroine's mind, and, although the narrative voice and Elinor's presumed thoughts are not always identical – Elinor is often displayed as acting through disappointment and anger as much as reason – the narrator does not encourage us to feel superior to her. As it develops, the story is told more and more through Elinor, given the kind of waspish opinions associated with the narrator: Robert Ferrars provides a face 'of strong, natural, sterling insignificance', while in his mother and sister she spies 'mean-spirited folly'. Elinor watches constantly and often judges correctly through looking at other people's eyes – to her the smitten Colonel Brandon reveals more through his gaze than through his social behaviour. Marianne studies Elinor for signs of love for Edward but fails to see through the surface of her reserve.

In the early sections of the novel the sisters spar rather like lovers, closer in dialogue to Darcy and Elizabeth in *Pride and Prejudice* than to Elizabeth and her sister Jane. Elinor is tart with Marianne in her grief over Willoughby's departure, perhaps in response to the indulgence displayed by their fond mother, and she reproaches Marianne with her own stoical example. In their period of anxiety and initial misery the sisters separate into secrecy and solitude. The distance is poignant because they are used to thinking each other's thoughts: Elinor imagines Marianne imagining Colonel Brandon's story, for example, and the imagined idea forms part of her own response. The sisters reunite when they grieve together, and both show extreme physical sensations at the suffering of the other. When Marianne receives the fatal letter from Willoughby she goes deathly pale, while Elinor sits in a tremor hardly able to hold up her head. When she reads the note Marianne collapses and 'almost choaked', then 'almost screamed', while Elinor gives 'way to a burst of tears, which at first were scarcely less violent than Marianne's'; when Edward becomes free, Marianne has hysterics and Elinor 'almost ran out of the room', then lets fall tears of joy. As the love affair of Marianne is seen primarily through Elinor's eyes, so Elinor's tentative love speeches are not to Edward but about Edward to Marianne.

The intensity of Marianne dominates a first reading of *Sense and Sensibility*, but a second may be more attuned to the interiority and suffering of Elinor. Partly because of her astringent habit of mind, the emphasis on her consciousness rather than Marianne's seems to subvert the lure of romance. Yet in romantic terms Elinor has much to reveal. The early stages of her loving are coolly delivered as the focus settles on her sister, but she is in fact the first to love. Only when she finds Edward free at the end does she show the emotion she has been repressing. And, like Colonel Brandon, she watches the beautiful Marianne, so gaining a semi-erotic involvement in her sister. In Burney's *Camilla*, the male lover constantly and oppressively studies his beloved, while in the most famous male sentimental novels, Henry Mackenzie's *The Man of Feeling*, Sterne's *A Sentimental Journey*, and Johann Wolfgang von Goethe's *The Sorrows of Young Werther*, the hero watches and responds to distress, in the best instances moving into empathy but also perhaps vicariously living and gratifying the self.

The passionate, erotically aroused side of Elinor comes to the fore in the scene when she encounters Willoughby while her sister lies ill. She has already shown she can be as romantically hoodwinked as Marianne when she imagined Lucy's hair hers and when she told her sister that nothing proved Edward 'unworthy', although it is surely 'unworthy' to gain the affections of one woman while engaged to another. Now again she lays herself open to delusion. Suitably, Willoughby arrives for seduction in a wild storm as he had on the first occasion, coming under the not unpleasing sensation that a beautiful girl is dying of love for him. Sensibility could be associated with delicate, female (sexualised) sickness: 'is not there something interesting to you in the flushed cheek, hollow eye, and quick pulse of a fever?' Elinor had once asked Marianne. Willoughby (like Brandon) is equally interested: after he repulsed her in the ballroom, he saw Marianne's deathlike face and now, 'when I thought of her to-day as really dying, it was a kind of comfort to me to imagine that I knew exactly how she would appear to those, who saw her last in this world' (S&S, 3:8). We know that Elinor has had a sleepless night, a day with hardly any food, and hours of acute anxiety; none the less it is a shock to find her responding thoroughly to Willoughby's words and 'manly beauty', to the glamour that had entranced her sister.

Willoughby has been seen and heard mainly in snatches through other people's perceptions; this is one of the few times he comes before us directly and our response may not equal that of the tired, emotional Elinor. His account of his dealings with Marianne and his plea for forgiveness are lamentable, but Elinor replies with compassion. Indeed, when later recollecting the scene, she translates his actual phrase, 'sincerely fond of her', into 'ardent love'. When, instead of remorse, he provides justification for his seduction, impregnation, and abandonment of Brandon's young ward of fifteen by claiming that she was as lusty as he and that he 'did not recollect' to give her his address, Elinor sees it as 'wanton cruelty' but does not turn from him in horror – even though he compares Eliza and Marianne in the warmth of their passion for him, so implying that their fates might have been similar. (Interestingly, his new wife is damned not for being indifferent to him but for again being passionately fond.) On very little evidence Elinor judges him 'naturally' honest but spoilt by the 'world', a plea she would not allow to Lucy Steele, equally needing to scheme for money. Willoughby is penitent because he has lost one of the things he wanted – a wife he was attracted to – the other being money, but even now he calls himself simply a 'rascal', using the word 'villain' only when he imagines Marianne fickle as well.

That night, Elinor again cannot sleep and her erotic fascination with her sister's faithless lover increases. She blames herself for being too harsh and worries about describing what happened, anxious 'whether after such an explanation [Marianne] could be happy with another'. She even 'for a moment wished Willoughby a widower' – presumably with his present wife's money. The encounter leaves the reader less convinced that Willoughby is capable of any romantic passion than that Elinor has romantic depths largely unrevealed. Her emotional commitment to Edward has influenced her response to Willoughby, and this is brought to the fore when he describes being forced to play the happy lover to another woman – Edward's situation with Lucy Steele, she supposes. Elinor accepts that a free Willoughby would have attractions no other man could have. Later, however, she reflects on the scene and realises that his main concern is not for loving but for making others love him.

When her sister recovers, Elinor reveals more of this emotionalism, but now interacting with the stoicism that so impresses Marianne:

> Elinor could not be cheerful. Her joy was of a different kind, and led to anything rather than to gaiety. Marianne restored to life, health, friends, and to her doating mother, was an idea to fill her heart with sensations of exquisite comfort, and expand it in fervent gratitude; – but it led to no outward demonstration of joy, no words, no smiles. All within Elinor's breast was satisfaction, silent and strong.   (*S&S*, 3:7)

Exquisite comfort

Marianne marries a man for whom she feels nothing more than esteem; in her sister's mind, she becomes a 'reward' for his suffering. Such a resolution upset readers from the start. Just after its publication Lady Bessborough found *Sense and Sensibility* amusing but thought 'it ends stupidly', while in the twentieth century Marvin Mudrick was outraged at the way Marianne is 'humiliated and destroyed', concluding, 'Marianne, the life and center of the novel, has been betrayed; and not by Willoughby.'[6] No such irritation inspires readers of *Northanger Abbey* when Henry Tilney marries Catherine from gratitude.

The uneasiness is partly due to the perfunctory close, brought about through a question (the unsettling technique will recur in Austen): 'With such a confederacy against her . . . what could she do?' so suggesting things might have been otherwise, and the final union of Marianne and Brandon is inevitably shadowed by the lost one of Marianne and Willoughby. Partly, too, it may be owing to an expectation of passion in women and to Austen's emphasis on Marianne's constant and active disdain for the middle-aged colonel with his flannel waistcoat. But perhaps help may come from a closer look both at the nature of romantic passion and at the depiction of Colonel Brandon, who does more in the book than own a suitably unimproved property and complete the structural pattern.

In its exclusiveness and self-destruction, passion usually implies tragedy. Here, in comedy, Austen accommodates it in all its psychological realism through portraying it in a second heroine who is not the central consciousness. So the romance can be seen from outside, combining glamour, seduction, absurdity, illusion, and danger. This last shows itself in addiction, for romance can become a form of disease, expressed in both bodily infirmity and alienation from the world. Marianne's fever, brought on not directly by passion but by passionate ignoring of the body's warning signs, suggests a loss of the usual human instinct for self-preservation.

Ironically, her recovery is signalled by her response to the passion of someone else as addicted and fantastical as herself. Colonel Brandon reinforces the notion that passion is, in Hume's words, a 'modification of existence, and contains not any representative quality, which renders it a copy of any other existence or modification'.[7] In other words, this kind of feeling never achieves an explanation commensurate with itself. The melancholy Colonel Brandon has loved romantically, even intending an elopement in his youth until thwarted, and, while not dying of his experience, he has let it take hold of his life and reduce him to despair, then settled depression. All this despite holding a pretty low opinion of its object, the first Eliza – he is rather shocked that she did not die of love for him, but went on living until a more ignominious end. As Marianne and Elinor project their desire on to their men, Colonel Brandon, with far less justification, projects his on to Marianne, made to reincarnate his lost love – a passionate instance of the novel's habit of duplication. Rather chillingly he then routes his new passion through memory. This manoeuvre will be developed in the later novels in the consciousness of Austen's heroines, especially Anne Elliot in *Persuasion*.

By the time he encounters Marianne in London, Brandon knows of Willoughby's seduction and betrayal of his ward Eliza and he joins the two women, for young Eliza has 'an affection for him as strong, still as strong as [Marianne's], and with a mind tormented by self-reproach, which must attend her through life'. As with *Northanger Abbey*, a second reading of *Sense and Sensibility* modifies our judgement. It allows the reader to discern that much of Brandon's gravity comes from his inner debate on whether to speak out and (probably uselessly) warn Marianne. This awareness makes Marianne's contempt for him more painful. He delivers his passionate anxiety in the broken speech and typographical excess of sentiment, so mocked in the *Juvenilia* when assumed by the unfeeling: 'My object – my wish – my sole wish in desiring it – I hope, I believe it is – is to be a means of giving comfort – no, I must not say comfort – not present comfort' (*S&S*, 2:9).

When Colonel Brandon looks at Marianne, he sees the trajectory of the first and second Elizas. He accepts that, for the young woman he loves, sensibility and sexuality are joined and that each Eliza is Marianne. When he sees the 'fervent . . . attachment of your sister to Mr. Willoughby', he discerns that of the 'lovely, blooming, healthful girl' who was brought to disgrace, sickness, and death through thwarted passion. In keeping with the tragic, romantic view of life, when he found his lost love, he assumed that 'Life could do nothing for her, beyond giving time for a better preparation for death.' When he later sees Marianne, saved, but only just, through friends and family from part of Eliza's fate, he still discerns Eliza in the 'altered looks . . . pale hand . . . hollow eye, the sickly skin, the posture of reclining weakness'. Eliza, it seems, would have been identical to Marianne had she been guarded 'by a firmer mind, or an happier marriage', both of which he offers at the conclusion of the novel. Only in this way will he compensate for his failure to guard the second Eliza. Ironically, he is going to rescue the romantic Marianne from her romantic propensities – when it is these, the youthful warmth and sexual candour, that attract him. To Elinor's sardonic amusement, her incorrigible mother declares that Marianne could not have been happy with Willoughby, who had 'something about the eyes' she did not like, while by now Elinor feels his allure. Brandon does not have Willoughby's sexual magnetism but Mrs Dashwood sees in him the passionate romantic nature that Willoughby lacks and Marianne herself displays.

If the marriage fulfils the romantic passion of one partner, what can it mean for the other? Before the close, the intensity of Marianne's initial dislike of the colonel is moderated by her own experience of disappointed love. Early on, Elinor joked that her sister is only impressed by misery and romance and, on cue, Marianne does soften a little to Brandon when she hears of his sensitive sufferings. But it is through Elinor above all that she shifts in attitude. Despite the titular antithesis, Elinor loves enthusiastically, but she tries to do so without the self-destructive aspects of love, the abandonment to the fictional, mental fantasy of a single perfect man that controls Marianne's perception. There are not many mentions of religion in Austen but it is implied here in the caveat against giving up the self entirely for another: it is 'not meant . . . not fit' if one is a Christian. When she recovers from illness, Marianne sees that, had she died, it would have been self-destruction and she admits to a 'desire to live' for a different kind of love – of God and family. Willoughby cannot be forgotten but he can be contained 'by religion, by reason, by constant employment'. It is often remarked that Marianne's illness silences her, but there is no complete change as there would be in a sentimental novel. She had already been mentally struck by Elinor's example, insisting that she would now exist only for her family: 'From you, from my home, I shall never again have the smallest incitement to move.' It was her usual exaggeration.

In place of erotic obsession comes a quality complexly presented in the novel: esteem, an emotion Willoughby seems unable to feel for any woman. Elinor begins here with Edward and holds to it even when reviewing his foolishness. Marianne, who once expected to fall sacrifice to an 'irresistible passion', then assumed she would face eternal spinsterhood, finally marries with strong 'esteem'; love follows, we are told, while nostalgia for the first romance informs each partner. Viewed from this perspective, the book values and regrets the loss of romantic passion but celebrates slow-growing love, allowing it to incorporate romantic memory.

In *A Vindication of The Rights of Woman*, Wollstonecraft thought women enslaved by sensibility, 'a romantic unnatural delicacy of feeling', so that they remained always childlike and deliciously dependent on men rather than on themselves. However, in her final work, *The Wrongs of Woman*, and in her personal letters she also saw the illusory feeling of heightened experience as valuable, even when it led to misery. Wollstonecraft herself provides a parallel for Marianne rather than Elinor. In 1798, just after her death, her husband had lovingly and unwisely published his *Memoir* of her, in which he declared her sincerity, enthusiasm, and probity and presented her to the world as the representative of sensibility. At the same time, he told of her illicit love affair with Gilbert Imlay, which had ended tragically. Jane Austen does not mention Wollstonecraft in her extant letters – she was a byword for impropriety after Godwin's publication – but there is little doubt that Austen knew of her, both personally through acquaintances and publicly as an icon of the revolutionary years.[8] She would not have approved her sexual activity, but in the portrait of Marianne she provides something of the generous and trusting aspects of the Wollstonecraft of the *Memoirs*.

Although more extreme, describing two suicide attempts rather than a suicidal illness, Godwin's narrative follows a similar trajectory to Marianne's. But, where Godwin presents closeness to death as part of Wollstonecraft's powerful sensibility, Austen suggests how culturally overwhelmed Marianne is by expectations of female passion leading to death. The two narratives come together again in the conclusion: after 'suffering some of the sharpest struggles that our nature is capable of enduring', Wollstonecraft saw her later and final love for Godwin as one of esteem, of 'sublime tranquillity'.[9]

Chapter 5

Pride and Prejudice

The slow and ponderous beginning of *Sense and Sensibility*, which details the Norland family, the estate and its entail, contrasts with the theatrical *tour de force* of *Pride and Prejudice*'s opening, which mimics Samuel Johnson's mocking generalisations on the human condition – 'It is a truth universally acknowledged, that a single man in possession of a good fortune, must be in want of a wife.' There follows a quick antiphonal dialogue expressing the marriage of Mr and Mrs Bennet, comically at odds with what Austen later described in her 'Plan of a Novel' as usual novel style: 'Book to open with father and daughter conversing in long speeches.'[1] When talk ends, the method switches to direct narrative comment of the sort usually preceding conversation in fiction; it declares what the attentive reader has already concluded: that 'Mr Bennet' is an 'odd mixture of quick parts, sarcastic humour, reserve, and caprice' and his wife a woman 'of mean understanding, little information, and uncertain temper' whose 'business of . . . life' is to get her daughters married. But the reader should be on guard: the narrative voice limits itself. Not stressed is the absence of Mr Bennet's 'business of . . . life', the proper care of a father for his numerous and precariously placed family. Five unprepared girls about to make the choices that will determine their adult futures should be a father's 'business' – especially in the light of his own unsatisfactory marriage. The narrator will not be a crutch for inattentive reading.

Such different accounts

Jane Austen famously called *Pride and Prejudice* 'light & bright & sparkling' (*L*, p. 203). Together with its epigrammatic minimal style, this sparkle has made it probably the most reread novel in English. The comedy of the opening sequence permeates the book and, although much happens that could have pathetic, even tragic, consequences, disasters are more successfully averted here than in *Sense and Sensibility*, in part because of better luck – the father does not die – in part because the reader sees much through the eyes of a vivacious, essentially cheerful heroine. Elizabeth Bennet has a coolness and scepticism that allows her to accept foibles and common selfishness, and to see with some equability both love and lust growing and dying. Conversations are often as empty as in the other two early novels, but they are made more delicious by being refracted through the consciousness of the heroine and her sardonic father, while even the malevolence of gossip is defanged by the astringent acceptance that 'we live, but to make sport for our neighbours, and laugh at them in our turn'.

Like *Sense and Sensibility*, the novel portrays individuals negotiating personal needs with external social demands and internalised moral codes: using manners to control or mask inevitable egoism, they manipulate talk to gratify themselves. Here, however, the negotiation is less painful and more absurd – as well as more rewarding and wry. The love plot becomes the movement of two individuals towards marriage; it is also a progress towards civility, not the superficial sort which acted as a bulwark against pain in *Sense and Sensibility* but something more socially and personally valuable, based on understanding another's feelings and consequently one's own.[2]

'First Impressions' may have been drafted in 1796–7 when Jane Austen was in her early twenties.[3] Over the next years it was read by family members and perhaps altered extensively in the early 1800s. In her own words, Austen 'lopt & cropt' the work (*L*, p. 202), making a taut, spare text with few descriptions of person or place. Something of an earlier form may remain in the use of letters. Darcy's brings about the *éclaircissement* and is tied to events, for Elizabeth reads and rereads it so that her own response converses with the contents, and the document is not inert but forms part of a dramatic scene. Elizabeth is the heroine least overwhelmed by literature and its language, but this letter is treated as other heroines treat literary texts; she soon knows it by heart and it starts to work on her mind like her own experience. But the letters from Jane and Mr Collins, conveying information or displaying eccentricity, may be relics of an earlier epistolary mode. Similarly, the grotesque characters seem close to the types in the *Juvenilia* in their extreme or predictable oddity; even Mr Darcy at the beginning resembles the juvenile comic boasters when his haughtiness repulses the whole village. Like the early tales and *Northanger Abbey*, the novel plays with conventions of eighteenth-century sentimental romance: parental interference is parodied in Lady Catherine, and the usual external obstruction is replaced by internal doubt; instead of love at first sight, a convention of sentimental and gothic fiction (see Radcliffe's *Mysteries of Udolpho*) comes initial contempt and resentment.

Although there is less authorial placing of the heroine than in *Northanger Abbey* and *Sense and Sensibility*, the narrator in *Pride and Prejudice* only slowly and incompletely aligns with her consciousness and she sees a good deal outside.

Mr Collins's proposal to Charlotte Lucas, unheard and unimagined by her friend Elizabeth, is delivered in two facetiously succinct sentences:

> Miss Lucas perceived him from an upper window as he walked towards the house, and instantly set out to meet him accidentally in the lane. But little had she dared to hope that so much love and eloquence awaited her there.   (*P&P*, 1:22)

With such narrative help, the reader notes Charlotte's manoeuvres, while Elizabeth remains unaware or projects her own emotions on to her friend. Approved by her clever father, she cannot quite believe in judgement outside her own, so she rejects the notion that Charlotte, a plain 'well-educated young woman of small fortune', can be sincere in what she says and cunning in her moves. Even after the marriage to Mr Collins, she makes unwarranted assumptions that redeem Charlotte – and her own choice of her as companion: that her friend is avoiding her spouse or that 'home and her housekeeping, her parish and her poultry' will lose 'their charms'. Yet we later learn that Charlotte and Collins coincide in opinions, while no loyalty to Elizabeth prevents her telling her husband enough of Longbourn home life for him to assert that Lydia's 'licentiousness of behaviour' results from 'a faulty degree of indulgence'. Unadmired in her family, less physically attractive, and not sensitised by the wild matchmaking of an irrepressible mother, Charlotte has less self-esteem and independence than Elizabeth. She notes that the admirable frankness of the eldest Bennet daughters, cultivated in the bracing atmosphere of their father, may not be appropriate in the marriage game they have now entered. She warns Elizabeth not to let 'fancy for Wickham', the charming soldier, degrade her 'in the eyes of a man [Darcy] of ten times his consequence', and she points out correctly that Jane's serenity with Bingley may be misconstrued. For Charlotte, men are prey to be caught by predatory women, who must make an effort in the chase.

As with Charlotte, so with Wickham the narrator largely leaves the heroine (and reader) to her own judgement. In early meetings Elizabeth urges him into indiscretion about Darcy, indulging herself by repeating the latter's words out of their duelling context – 'I *do* remember his boasting one day at Netherfield, of the implacability of his resentments' – and declaring on short acquaintance that he is 'disagreeable' and 'ill-tempered', that 'Everybody is disgusted with his pride.' She knows that her prying into men's affairs is a 'weakness', but cannot resist. The sexual admiration of a handsome, agreeable man, compensating for Darcy's 'mortifying' scorn on their first meeting – he had said she was not beautiful enough to tempt him and he would not give 'consequence' to a woman spurned by others – makes her conclude of Wickham: 'there was truth in his looks'. She begins to fall in love without much questioning of herself or her object and she sets off to the Netherfield ball intending to conquer 'all that remained unsubdued of his heart'. Only his non-appearance stalls her and she blames Darcy for it. In all this there is little astringent narrative comment.

In fact, Wickham is just an old-fashioned rake and charmer, the adaptable eighteenth-century type of hero now giving way to a more earnest ideal of understated emotion – the type represented by Darcy.[4] But Wickham has other attractions for Elizabeth. His equivalents in Austen novels, Willoughby and Captain Tilney, are well born; Wickham is more clearly an outsider, immune to social demands. Elizabeth's favourable response to him is in part because she assumes that she and he are equal and alike: a woman and a dependent man making common cause against the 'stateliness of money and rank'. Unlike Miss Bingley, she is unperturbed by Wickham's lowly birth – it is, after all, equivalent to her mother's.

We will recollect what we have seen

In *Sense and Sensibility* Colonel Brandon was dominated by memory of his past, while Willoughby, whose initial cruelty included his not 'recollecting' to give his address to young Eliza, avoids memory as much as he can. In *Mansfield Park* Fanny Price describes the faculty as '*more* wonderful' than all others; here in *Pride and Prejudice*, however, it becomes malleable and yields up the past to present desires, so that even Mrs Gardiner, Elizabeth's sensible aunt, can deceive herself. Impressed with Wickham and needing to justify his dislike of Darcy, she becomes 'confident at last that she recollected having heard Mr Fitzwilliam Darcy formerly spoken of as a very proud, ill-natured boy'; in fact she remembers nothing of him.

Darcy fears that Elizabeth lives only in the present and indeed, like most Austen heroines with the exception of Anne Elliot and possibly Fanny Price, this *is* her natural home. Playfully she urges control of memory: 'Think only of the past as its remembrance brings you pleasure' (*P&P*, 3:16). But Darcy believes the past holds truth and is fixed, not subject to such easy choice – hence his attitude to Wickham, who has done him immense wrong (wasting opportunities given by Darcy's father and trying to seduce his young sister), and he determines to have nothing to do with Wickham in future. He believes that a person cannot and should not entirely control memory; the struggle to improve oneself demands as clear an assessment of one's past as possible, even if this recollected past can never be entirely accurate.

Memory fits with the novel's investigation of vision and revision. When the northern pleasure trip is suggested by her aunt Gardiner, Elizabeth declares she will be precise about what she sees. Yet the tiresome Mr Collins is also accurate: he numbers each field and tree and shows his ground 'with a minuteness which left beauty entirely behind'. Clearly, aesthetic processing of the sort Catherine was learning too fully in *Northanger Abbey* is also required to see well – what is seen and remembered is filtered through personality, cultural knowledge, and expectation.

Seeing the self is more complex. When Elizabeth exclaims, 'Till this moment, I never knew myself', she is reacting to another person's viewpoint about herself and her past and is most contingent. What she has seen is not some essential fixed self but the excessive power of self-indulgent judgement – or prejudice – within her. So the moment is not the end of a journey into self-knowledge but rather a stage in a process of viewing herself – and of the reader viewing her. Observation on which she prided herself had told her little, especially when guided by feeling, by experience of rejection and admiration – she had simply needed better information. Elizabeth is a splendid talker, hence her great appeal; she is less accomplished as a listener. 'Prejudice' is shown to be the result of indiscriminate interacting as well as self-absorption. But the book veers from absolute judgements; in the end nothing is 'universally acknowledged' – except perhaps human fallibility.

The title *Pride and Prejudice* was probably an allusion to the ending of Frances Burney's *Cecilia* where the miseries suffered by hero and heroine are said to have been 'the result of PRIDE and PREJUDICE' (vol. 5, bk 10, ch. 10). But the phrase is common in the eighteenth century and draws the book into the philosophical discussion of human nature. In *Reflections* Burke had recently invested the notion of 'prejudices' with unusual value as part of a nation's hold on identity – 'we cherish them because they are prejudices' – and of an individual's path to virtue. 'Prejudice', he wrote, 'renders a man's virtue his habit; and not a series of unconnected acts.'[5] Hume and the philosopher Adam Smith explored the notion of 'pride' as self-esteem: although essential, pride harms when it blinds a person to his or her own character or when, in Elizabeth's phrase, it 'mortified' another's.[6] Pride and prejudice start to sound remarkably alike.

Hume thought that 'haughty indolence' resulted from too great a contemplation of 'pedigrees and genealogies'.[7] Darcy is proud of his rank at the top of the gentry and, when he attacks her vulgar family, Elizabeth bridles at the insult to her lower status. She does the same when Lady Catherine scorns her, taking her stand not on universal equality but on equality within the gentry. In time, Darcy comes to appreciate that a 'gentleman' is a person of merit and manners rather than rank alone, while Elizabeth accepts his 'pride' as natural – as the worldly Charlotte always considered it. She rejects her earlier sense of resemblance between him and his awful aunt Lady Catherine. Now she ascribes Darcy's rescue of her foolish sister Lydia in part to proper 'pride', when, as her aunt and uncle surmise, it comes primarily from love.

Elizabeth sees more of herself as she sees more of Darcy, the knowledge coming less from conversations than from visual images. At Pemberley she approaches him through his house, grounds, housekeeper's discourse, and portrait, all seen through newly tinted spectacles. Before Darcy consciously interested her, Elizabeth found herself attending to talk of Pemberley, 'that noble place' which Bingley declares inimitable. As she draws near on her Derbyshire tour, 'her spirits were in a high flutter', a word used for Marianne when sexually excited. So, where she was ready for pretentiousness at Rosings, here she is prepared to let the ancestral house and grounds, neither 'formal nor falsely adorned', charm her. Despite her intention to register things minutely, Pemberley appears to Elizabeth – and therefore the reader – in generalised terms, gaining some of its mystique through implied comparisons with noisy Longbourn, empty Netherfield Park, and ostentatious, even 'kitsch', Rosings.[8]

The estate speaks to Elizabeth of other sorts of existence. Hume had demonstrated his aesthetic theory about sympathy as the source of ideas of beauty through an analogy with a country house tour. He believed that our pleasure in such a tour consists in 'our sympathizing with the proprietor of the lodging'. Adela Pinch applied this notion to Pride and Prejudice: 'after viewing the structure of the house we are led to admire its contents, then its grounds, and finally the personal advantages of the man himself. The train of our sympathies, that is, cause the figure of an individual to emerge in the text, personified through feeling – he is in his own elegant house: he is a man whose sense of self is constituted by his qualities, his extensive objects and, in particular, the esteem of others.'[9] At Pemberley Elizabeth sees Darcy controlling grateful servants, fish, trees, lakes, and lands. She notes unruptured order and mastery and finds them erotic. There will be far more about the creation and maintenance of an estate in the later books – Mansfield Park and Emma. Here Pemberley just resplendently is, not just private property but a metonym for its owner and his allure.

Inside the house, the Gardiners retain the scepticism that is leaving Elizabeth, suspecting the housekeeper's praise as the usual servile devotion. Their niece 'doubted' but was 'impatient for more'. As she had been imposed on by Wickham, she is now happy to be imposed on by the housekeeper. While Darcy himself is an absent presence, she comes to 'own' Pemberley by listening to stories and gazing on the house, taking possession in imagination – rather as humble Fanny Price does in *Mansfield Park* when she comes to love 'this house and everything in it'. This possessive viewing legitimates Elizabeth's upward social movement to mistress-ship and the half-mocking speech to Jane, that her growing love derived from her 'first seeing [Darcy's] beautiful grounds at Pemberley', echoes inner thought and images.

Catherine Morland had mistakenly expected to read something from Mrs Tilney's picture; in Pemberley before Darcy's portrait Elizabeth trusts a likeness even over her own experience, or rather she invests this likeness with reordered memory. She had earlier had difficulty making her own 'portrait' of Darcy; here she helps an external work by giving it Darcy's now known feeling for her – its smile becomes one 'she remembered to have sometimes seen when he looked at her', a memory rather at odds with what the reader has heard. Instead simply of contemplating the portrait, Elizabeth gives it agency, making it fix its 'eyes upon herself'. The combined images of grounds, house, discourse, and painting envelop Darcy in the glamour of power, the kind of power she had earlier found disturbing when used to degrade her and dismiss her sister: 'gentle sensations' follow from the idea that 'many people's happiness were in his guardianship'. The gift of himself, so crudely offered, becomes valuable: she thinks of 'his regard with a deeper sentiment of gratitude than it had ever raised before'. To be desired by this sort of landowner becomes 'something'. There is comedy in this acceptance of the erotic charm of social significance, but judgement is difficult and anything is grist to its mill.

When the real Darcy crashes through the stylised images she has been contemplating, Elizabeth's first response is not her usual pertness but shame at the sight she must present to him: a woman pursuing him, a middle-class tourist on an upper-class estate accompanied by relatives 'in a low way, in trade', as Emma, a later heroine, expresses it. Although managing a 'sly' look at Darcy's response to the Gardiners of Cheapside, she is predominantly 'astonished and confused'. Later, when she sees Darcy and his sister coming to the inn in their carriage, she responds with a 'discomposure' which amazes her, while on learning of Lydia's flight her knees tremble and she dissolves into tears. Then she learns that her sister's misbehaviour has not ruined her chances and discovers that her display of feminine distress has done her no harm. In *Mansfield Park* Mary Crawford will conspicuously fail to follow her in feminine 'discomposure' at a similarly testing moment.

I dearly love a laugh

As even the Pemberley episode suggests, Elizabeth's family legacy is central to *Pride and Prejudice*. Mrs Bennet may be shameless, scheming, clumsy, and absurd but (especially before Darcy's proposal) there are resemblances, unnoticed by Elizabeth, between her and her clever but still young and impressionable daughter. With her mother and her mother's favourite, the sexually irrepressible Lydia, Elizabeth finds the selfish Wickham seductive. Significantly, the flirtation flourishes under the eyes of Mrs Bennet and within her sister's vulgar circle at Meryton. Despite Darcy's infatuated praise, like her mother Elizabeth may at times seem 'ill bred': to the incivility of the Bingley sisters, who exclude her as they take their walk, Elizabeth responds by naughtily citing Gilpin's remark on the picturesque quality of trios – knowing the reference is to arranged cows. At Rosings, she mocks the parade of aristocracy by boasting of her own uncontrolled family and counters the inflated awe of the Lucases by comparing the excitement caused by Miss De Bourgh's arrival to that generated by pigs getting into a garden. Like her mother she wants to win an argument, and the two women come uncomfortably together when Mrs Bennet exposes her vulgarity by supporting her daughter in her contest with Darcy by insisting on the scandalous merits of country society.

Elizabeth and Lydia are the laughers of the family. When Miss Bingley insists that Darcy is a man at whom one cannot laugh, Elizabeth responds in the tones of her father: 'That is an uncommon advantage, and uncommon I hope it will continue, for it would be a great loss to *me* to have many such acquaintance. I dearly love a laugh' (*P&P*, 1:11). Lydia's laughter is more sexy and disruptive and it haunts all of them: 'You will laugh when you know where I am gone, and I cannot help laughing myself at your surprise to morrow morning, as soon as I am missed' (*P&P*, 3:5), she writes, as she flies off to what would be certain ruin had her sister's more restrained humour not captured a powerful man. Mr Bennet knows the sexual aspects of laughter when he fears that his laughing, mocking, favourite daughter, marrying without love, could also go astray.

Lady Catherine could not be more wrong when she remarks, 'Daughters are never of so much consequence to a father', for Mr Bennet has made Elizabeth almost a substitute wife, a 'partner in his pleasure', the person with whom he expects to exchange private glances on public occasions, enjoy his perceptive flippancy and accept his harsh vision of the world. She is to join him in looking at life as entertainment, a way of distancing painful truths and avoiding emotional involvement. He invites her to indulge in unwise mockery of his heir Mr Collins, whose takeover of Longbourn becomes something to be laughed at rather than anxiously anticipated. It culminates in his staged reaction to Mr Collins's proposal; Elizabeth colludes: she 'could not but smile'. As with General Tilney and Henry, there are uncomfortable resemblances between parent and worthier child.

Mr Bennet has little notion of his daughter as a vulnerable adult. The first two chapters delay Elizabeth's entry and portray her first of all as member of a numerous family of girls. Despite her quickness, she is, as 'little Lizzy', subsumed in her father's refreshing but alarming generalisation of his children as 'silly and ignorant'. She moves to the centre when the narrator echoes Mr Bennet's perception that she has 'more quickness of observation' than the others. The typical young woman will, however, surface intermittently through the book, as when, dancing at Netherfield with her uncouth cousin, Elizabeth feels 'shame and misery', then the 'exstasy' of release – rather like Catherine Morland escaping John Thorpe. In response to her serious warning over Lydia's conduct, Mr Bennet reduces his daughter to a child again, calling her 'Poor little Lizzy!' and imagining her suitors as 'squeamish youths'. Despite seeing through Wickham, Mr Bennet lets him dine often at Longbourn and mingle with his daughters in 'general unreserve', and he equably watches the growing and unconcealed affection of Elizabeth for him.

At home Mr Bennet has encouraged his daughter's spirited talk – Mrs Bennet describes her running on 'in a wild manner' – and he gives her no guidance in behaviour outside. From such habits she has developed a saucy flirtatiousness or 'easy playfulness' quite at odds with conduct-book advice and appalling to Lady Catherine, while it attracts and disturbs Darcy. She has also copied her father's habit of exploiting embarrassment or social discomfort for its humour: 'with great spirit' Elizabeth makes a comic story of Darcy's rudeness at the Meryton ball and by so doing jokes about what must have stung her, for the fastidious comment is more appalling to her than for the reader who hears it in the context of Bingley's gushing enthusiasm for *all* the pretty girls. Her comic tale keeps Darcy and his affront alive in her and other people's memories. She goes to Rosings rather as her father went to Netherfield, with some expectation of being amused, and consequently she pricks the pretensions of Lady Catherine. She is stopped in this career only when Darcy more seriously hurts her self-esteem with his corrosive attack on her family.

Yet there are differences between father and daughter. Both enjoy their superiority to others but Mr Bennet gets inappropriate pleasure in baiting, while never trying to reform, his obtuse wife and in exposing the awkwardness, discomfort, and vulgarity of his family to outsiders – at Netherfield he is described as 'enjoying the scene' of their humiliation. He is happy to have Elizabeth as audience of his wit but, where her wit remains social, his can be enjoyed solipsistically. Indeed, his indulgence and habits of privileged retirement in his library, the only rational space in the house, combine to make him no longer entirely suited to sensible company. Late in the novel the narrator gives the expected prehistory: Mr Bennet, a landowner of £2,000 a year, was captivated by youth, beauty, and an appearance of good humour, and, having married a wife with weak understanding, lost all 'respect, esteem, and confidence' as well as the possibility of domestic happiness. (Yet Mrs Bennet remains proud of her grumpy spouse: when Darcy scorns Elizabeth, she wishes Mr Bennet had been there 'to have given him one of your set-downs', while his solace may be the good dinners he regularly eats.)

The prehistory bases Mr Bennet's indolence and cynicism on disappointment. Occasionally in the novel it approaches bleakness, as when he composedly contemplates Jane's death in pursuit of Mr Bingley and his own as signifying nothing more than financial ruin for his family. *Real* bleakness emerges only twice: on receiving the letter detailing Lydia's rescue without his aid, he does not bother even to tell his wife and rudely orders his daughters from his library. The other occasion is more anguished; after Elizabeth declares her wish to marry Darcy, her father blurts out: 'My child, let me not have the grief of seeing *you* unable to respect your partner in life. You know not what you are about' (*P&P*, 3:17).

Lydia's elopement tests and then deposes Mr Bennet, for Wickham's action presupposes an impotent father. After creating so many scenes to amuse himself, for a while he faces real crisis with 'excessive distress'. But the family looks for practical help to Mr Gardiner, and Mr Bennet fails even to do his duty of reporting back when he goes to London. On his return, despite for a time realising that 'It has been my own doing, and I ought to feel it', he is largely unchanged. Soon he is again forming little humorous scenes, imagining himself mimicking his wife by giving 'as much trouble as I can' or providing gothic imprisonment for stupid Kitty. Knowing the result of his inadequate marriage and withdrawal from his family, he yet continues amused with his own wit; even the statement of shame has to be mocking: 'let me once in my life feel how much I have been to blame. I am not afraid of being overpowered by the impression.' Self-knowledge cannot withstand his habit of mind and he continues to treat his more foolish daughters with sarcasm, and mock the mother whose authority he has allowed to damage them. Crisis averted, he reverts to his stance of detached amusement and 'open pleasantry', so that only Mrs Gardiner is left uselessly preaching moral sense to Lydia.

Mr Bennet is an appealing and troubling figure, in many ways at the opposite spectrum from the autocrat General Tilney, who attempts to control every aspect of his children's lives. Lacking the wit to gloss his shortcomings, the general is usually perceived as the greater failure although his parenting exposes his children to fewer risks. The critique of a patriarch is reasonable enough in the context of Fielding or Richardson, who present such powerful figures as dangerous in mid-eighteenth-century society. But, left unreformed and to some extent abandoned at the end, Mr Bennet is subversive in the context of the politicised 1790s. Radical works, like those of Godwin and Tom Paine, saw reverence for the patriarch as irrational prejudice and social slavery, while the conservative novels of More and West overtly defended filial duty against this radical challenge and roundly condemned any mockery of the parent–child tie. For modern readers, Mr Bennet may disturb in a different way. Although he is undercut by the narrative, we cannot avoid enjoying his amoral verbal cleverness. Indeed, he seems close to the author, for he too is a kind of fictionist.

Elizabeth's attitude to her family modulates with Darcy's letter, internalised through repeated rereadings. Properly realising his passion for her, however crudely and cruelly expressed, she begins to overcompensate for her earlier poor opinion by accepting almost all his views. She acknowledges that her family's failings are more than 'ridiculous'. Although the narrator claimed that Elizabeth had 'never been blind to the impropriety of her father's behaviour as a husband', only now does she see it as a 'continual breach of conjugal obligation and decorum which, in exposing his wife to the contempt of her own children, was so highly reprehensible' (*P&P*, 2:19). Like a parent with an unsatisfactory child she feels 'disappointed and sorry' for her father.

Now she questions those qualities she shares with Mr Bennet, the turns of phrase and even temperament: 'I meant to be uncommonly clever in taking so decided a dislike to [Mr Darcy], without any reason', she tells Jane. Even her manner becomes problematic to her: 'my spirits might often lead me wrong'. The pert remarks she made to Lady Catherine about all her sisters being uneducated and 'out' give way to a realisation that Lydia, abandoned to 'amusement and vanity', may ruin them all. With her mind and memory corrected – perhaps excessively so – by the tones of Darcy's letter, she meets Kitty and Lydia unchaperoned in an inn (compare Eleanor Tilney's horror at Catherine travelling home alone) and feels to the quick the impropriety of her family. She listens with distaste to the kind of spiritedly coarse talk their mother allowed, knowing that, despite her own fastidiousness, the 'coarseness of the *sentiment*' was hers. Darcy is superseding her father as internal monitor – arguably one patriarchal authority replaces another. When Lydia's visit to the militia in Brighton is mooted, Elizabeth lies to Mr Bennet about the possible influence on her own 'squeamish' suitor but regards the event as 'the death warrant' of 'commonsense'. She is not now amused at her family's scene-painting, Lydia of herself as camp sweetheart, her father of Lydia as lunatic public exhibit. Here Lydia functions like Lady Catherine, for both women allow their superior relatives, Darcy and Elizabeth, to see unworthy family aspects in them rather than in themselves.

As her manners and attitudes suggest, with no guidance except what her aunt Gardiner occasionally gives her, Elizabeth has been too little aware of the realities of the marriage market she is entering. Hence her desire to have the penniless Wickham as lover because he appeals to her. She mocks Darcy's undervaluing of her beauty although it is a necessary asset in the marketplace. Darcy's remark is followed by Mr Collins's proposal, which includes mention of her lack of portion; this precedes Darcy's proposal, providing comments on her prejudicial family. The funniest scene of the novel, Mr Collins's formal proposal delivered with extravagance in stock sentimental rhetoric, every word of which exposes his offer as a business matter, is mirrored by Darcy's unconventional and open declaration of genuine desire. At first sight so very different, the two suitors share a self-confident belief in the success of their offers – symptom of the cultural mastery accorded to men. The parallel proposals teach Elizabeth much about her condition and, after reading Darcy's letter, she views herself clearly as a marriageable woman with disadvantages: 'she felt depressed beyond anything she had ever known [before]'. If she is to become a wife she must rein in the ebullience and libido she shares with Lydia.

How ardently I admire and love you

Yet the very aspects of herself that derived from her unsatisfactory family and now 'shame' her have attracted the fastidious Darcy, initially proof against her beauty, sisterly love, and other feminine virtues. Not dwelling on 'vexation' (at missing Wickham), she appears engagingly cheerful at the Netherfield ball and Darcy interprets her 'easy playfulness' as both refreshing indifference and, paradoxically, interest in himself. Her irritation fuels repartee, as she follows Henry Tilney in 'archly' demanding the formulaic utterances of the ballroom. So she forms herself and Darcy into a theatrical pair, the Shakespearean witty lovers or the 'gay couple' of Restoration comedy. Darcy enjoys the flirtatious – even racy – attention she gives him, often with the sting of unusual criticism in its tail.

Although Lydia's ebullient laughter has been so destructive and although Elizabeth learns to curb hers around Darcy – he 'had yet to learn to be laught at', she muses, stifling a remark about his gratifying friendship with the pliable Bingley – and despite all her expressed shame at herself and her family, laughter remains a boasted habit. When all is settled, Elizabeth declares her happiness in laughter. Darcy is both charmed and alarmed by this habit. He feels it degrades what should be serious and in the exchanges of wit with Elizabeth he often smiles when bested or when his masculine power is usurped, but does not laugh. We later surmise that his gravity had propelled his young sister into the arms of a more trivial man. Yet, despite his keen sense of the impropriety of laughter, he finds himself attracted to the sort of ungenteel and brisk woman disparaged by Fordyce and Hannah More as prelude to libertine disaster. He sees the erotic freedom of Elizabeth's wit, her taking charge of the dance and her laughing with his cousin in his aunt's stuffy drawing room. It fits with her equally disturbing and attractive physical energy, her jumping over stiles near her home, springing over puddles, and ending with dirty clothes and glowing face.[10]

To keep the emphasis on Elizabeth, Darcy as desiring subject is seen mainly through her flickering gaze as she responds to his response to her and to others' responses to him. In fact, both are presented as not really seeing the other at all. Following the lesson of her father, Elizabeth wrongly imposes on Darcy a 'very satirical eye', while he takes her arch looks and domineering comic speech – which Miss Bingley sees as 'bordering on conceit and impertinence' – as an effort to 'bewitch' him: as a result he assumes Elizabeth is 'expecting his addresses'. When he falls romantically in love, he is obsessed with his own feelings and hardly sees his beloved as he comically inverts the opening sentence of the book, that a single woman must always want a 'man in possession of a good fortune'.

Darcy has no damascene conversion after Elizabeth's refusal and he is still 'surprised' at relations from Cheapside. Only later does the reader learn that he has been 'tortured' by her taunt that he was no 'gentleman', that vague cultural notion that both she and he so deeply respect. He comes to realise he has insufficient inner capital to tempt Elizabeth when he offers only his rich carapace – whose value paradoxically she herself is now starting to understand. He makes an effort to break out of his rank-inflected prejudices and see merit where it can be found, thus achieving 'gentlemanly' civility: so, although arriving at Pemberley as tourists, the Gardiners soon find themselves guests despite the taint of trade. Elizabeth now suspects the erotic fascination she holds for Darcy, but not its extent. When he leaves her after hearing of Lydia's disgrace, she assumes he has left because of this further example of her family's failings, where he has, in fact, understood that Elizabeth cannot be divorced from this family – and that, in human terms, what she offers is not much worse than what he brings, an almost disgraced sister and an impertinent aunt. (He has also seen, from her response to Lydia's action, that her laughing spirits can be curbed and do not portend immorality.) Each has influenced the other through passionate words: hers in response to his first proposal and his in his letter. So began the process of internal change.

Where the heroine's mind is sometimes caught in passages of internal monologue, Darcy's implied feeling has to erupt in sudden direct speech. A tendency to be reticent about the consciousness of the desiring man contributes to the widespread notion that Austen is not a writer on human passions but Charlotte

Brontë's cold author. Yet Darcy's mounting obsession is clearly if succinctly delivered through comments on his secret 'admiration' and sense of 'danger', his insistence on repression, consequently his zigzag of desire between acceptance and denial. He is isolated, for, like his sister, he has no confidant. His friendship with Bingley is an unequal one: he even uses him to help distance himself from Elizabeth as he seeks to quash his friend's love for her sister Jane. He tries but fails to control his feeling with images of his beloved's awful mother and trading uncle, and the result is the rudeness of his proposal, born of anger at himself for his own desire. Here and throughout, his emotions are as close to sexual infatuation as Austen can reasonably come within the conventions of her day.

Like Emily Brontë's Heathcliff, Darcy has become a popular cultural icon, helped by screen adaptations where he can display himself not simply in brief talk and a lengthy analytical letter, but also through passionate gesture and tone. Darcy's erotic appeal transcends his activities in the book and is part and parcel of his masculine political and psychological power. Despite its insolent criticisms born of this assured power, his proposal has thrilled generations of readers with its unexpected intensity:

> In vain have I struggled. It will not do. My feelings will not be repressed. You must allow me to tell you how ardently I admire and love you.   (*P&P*, 2:11)

Darcy's overwhelming passionate desire for Elizabeth brings about the leap across rank – which, however, remains in place. Higher in status than any other Austen hero, he may not have a title but he arrives as almost a fantasy lord with his arrogant relations, Norman name, and huge estate. The glamour of aristocracy, criticised in the texture of the book and thoroughly exposed in the later novels, settles on him, so that the fable becomes one of power tamed but not made equal by love. Charlotte Lucas's commonsensical opinions about marriage draw attention to the romantic nature of the central courtship story and its delicious fable. Although much is made in Austen criticism of the upward social mobility of the lower-gentry or middle-class woman of superior understanding or sensibility, of bourgeois individualism taming aristocratic authority, it actually happens only here, in *Pride and Prejudice*. But so strong is the effect, so consonant with cultural fantasy and wish fulfilment, that this one novel often does duty for the whole Austen œuvre.

What makes the passion more beguiling is that it is one-sided, not from a prudential conduct-book belief that a woman should not show love before a man has declared it, but from the heroine's independence of spirit. The repeated notion of Elizabeth as mistress of Pemberley remains bathetic, however swathed in complexity or humour, and she is nowhere shown overcome with longing in the manner of Marianne or even Elinor. Indeed, her father's anxiety and her own coolness, together with the sense of mastery still clinging to Darcy, give a slight chill to the sunny end.[11] Elizabeth's post-proposal realisation that Darcy 'had yet to learn to be laught at' certainly suggests that her desire to challenge his controlling manner persists unabated; perhaps, more depressingly, it also indicates her continuing use of wit to avoid a deeper emotional commitment: with 'playfulness' being Elizabeth's most noted attribute, Austen's favourite romantic comedy in fact dismantles the myth (beloved of romantic and screwball comedy) of the concomitance of both sentiments – at least in one consciousness. Elizabeth has investigated her own feelings and not found infatuation among them; rather she reflects on her self and sees her interest and interests. She comes to 'affection' but never falls deeply in love. Despite the common perception that *Pride and Prejudice* is Austen's most satisfying romance, its final emotional configuration is much the same as the unequal alliance between Colonel Brandon and Marianne in *Sense and Sensibility*: infatuation on the man's part, gratitude on the woman's. The tendency of Elizabeth's mind is caught (rather bleakly) in the narrator's comment:

> If gratitude and esteem are good foundations of affection, Elizabeth's change of sentiment will be neither improbable nor faulty. But if otherwise, if the regard springing from such sources is unreasonable or unnatural, in comparison of what is so often described as arising on a first interview with its object, and even before two words have been exchanged, nothing can be said in her defence, except that she had given somewhat of a trial to the latter method, in her partiality for Wickham, and that its ill-success might perhaps authorise her to seek the other less interesting mode of attachment.   (*P&P*, 3:4)

Although part of the happy ending is the exclusion of Mrs Bennet from her elder daughters' lives, she was comically right when she declared of Jane, 'I was sure you could not be so beautiful for nothing.' Substituting cool wit for beauty, Mr Bennet might have said the same for Elizabeth.

Chapter 6

Mansfield Park

'I have something in hand – which I hope on the credit of P. & P. will sell well, tho' not half so entertaining', wrote Jane Austen in September 1813 (*L*, p. 217). Her decision not to repeat the 'entertaining' formula of her most successful book suggests that, in *Mansfield Park*, she was aiming at something beyond easy approval. The work opens with an intertextual allusion to *Pride and Prejudice*, which she was probably revising while writing the new book – 'There certainly are not so many men of large fortune in the world as there are pretty women to deserve them' – but the contrast of the two novels exceeds the resemblance. In *Mansfield Park* a greater sense of the influence of place and circumstance on the insecure personality diminishes the pure delight in comic character, while the sprightly dialogue of *Pride and Prejudice* disappears before purposeful discussion of clerical duties and land improvement.

The third novel to be published, *Mansfield Park* was the first to be started after Jane Austen had settled in Chawton and was establishing herself as a professional writer. It was printed by Egerton and then Murray, the move to this fashionable publisher confirming that its author was aiming less for circulating libraries than for buyers intending to keep and reread. Her authorship was becoming known: '[T]he truth is that the Secret has spread so far as to be scarcely the Shadow of a secret now', she wrote. 'I beleive whenever the 3^d appears, I shall not even attempt to tell Lies about it' (*L*, p. 231) – in fact she continued to guard the secret as much as she could. It is not absolutely clear when she began the work, in 1811 or 1812, but it was concluded in the summer of 1813. Unlike *Northanger Abbey*, for whose datedness she would later apologise, and despite some dispute about its precise time, it is intended as contemporary in reference and analysis. Austen was concerned to get right even peripheral details, seeking to know whether there was a Government or Commissioner's House in Gibraltar and whether Northampton had hedgerows.

Although many critics regard it as her supreme achievement, *Mansfield Park* is rarely anyone's favourite Austen work: its greatness equals its power to offend. In 1917 Reginald Farrer wrote: 'None of her books is quite so brilliant in parts, none shows a greater technical mastery, a more audacious facing of realities, a more certain touch with character. Yet, alone of her books, *Mansfield Park* is vitiated throughout by a radical dishonesty.'[1] With various modulations, later critics declare that here the moralist and creator are at odds, and that this troubling and challenging work defies satisfactory or 'comfortable' interpretation – to use one of the novel's key words – however remarkable its technical achievements. Where most of the novels seem almost effortlessly to meld Austen's creative urge to be funny and her aesthetic aim to represent individual ethical integrity with psychological faithfulness, *Mansfield Park* is resented for according predominance to morality at the cost of comedy and vigour: almost invariably the problem is the 'creep-mouse' heroine, Fanny Price, declared 'priggish' and 'morally detestable'. Moving only when propelled by masculine kindness, she is male-centred and victimised, revelling in abjection. Most troubling is her defeat of the alternative heroine, Mary Crawford, who, with her spirit and wit, appears a challenging version of the impudent and charming Elizabeth Bennet. In this defeat, the book seems 'to speak for repression and negation, fixity and enclosure'.[2] In some respects the novel itself resembles its heroine, and possibly the disappointment readers feel, coming to it from *Pride and Prejudice*, stems in part from the leisurely movement of the story: the opening focus on the development of a child's ponderous interiority. Perhaps Austen realised that she had tested her readers with her slow pace for, a few months after publication, in a letter suggesting changes to a niece's draft novel, she observed: 'One does not care for girls till they are grown up' (*L*, p. 276).

Principle, active principle

When composing the novel, Jane told Cassandra that she was reading 'an Essay on the Military Police [Policy] & Institutions of the British Empire, by Capt. Pasley of the Engineers' and finding it 'delightfully written & highly entertaining' (*L*, p. 198). She was, she declared, 'much in love with the Author'. Pasley was a paternalistic imperialist, but his main purpose in his book was not to encourage empire but to rally the despondent British at a particularly depressing moment in their struggle against France – or 'thraldom' as he termed defeat and invasion by Napoleon, very much possibilities when he wrote. He felt his countrymen had lost their will to win the long-drawn-out conflict: 'War should not be lightly entered into, nor should any warlike enterprise be rashly undertaken', he wrote, 'but when once undertaken, those who have drawn the sword should never give way to despair, on account of difficulties or dangers, foreseen or not foreseen. The art of war is the art of surmounting difficulties, and of setting danger at defiance.'[3]

Moral purpose in the home and nation was essential to the war effort. In *Mansfield Park*, Austen presents the military and the Church as the two serious professions that potentially support the country in a difficult and sapping time, the one defending it abroad, the other stiffening moral fibre at home and establishing those principles for which men were fighting. These 'active' principles are what the book's patriarch Sir Thomas Bertram finds lacking in most of the inhabitants of Mansfield Park, but which his niece Fanny Price, with her fortuitous conjunction of humility and self-esteem, 'struggles' to hold, while falling victim to their perversion in her uncle. He himself is compromised not only by his presumed ownership of slaves in Antigua (the disordered colonial plantations may be linked to disorder in the English home) but primarily by his insidious arrogance, which allows him to treat his family as commodities.[4]

The moral deficiency within Mansfield Park is adumbrated in the sardonic opening of the first chapter, where the three middle-class Ward sisters are assessed in monetary not moral terms by their mercenary lawyer uncle and enter into a lifetime of sexual and social rivalry. The eldest two marry Sir Thomas Bertram and the Reverend Mr Norris respectively, with no mention of love but much concern for money, one responding to an advantageous offer, the other to a 'not contemptible' one. The third marries a lowly lieutenant of marines, presumably for love and no money, so disobliging her family. All lack balance between prudence and romance, love and self-interest. The result is poor parenting in two of the couples, with the dissatisfied, childless sister Mrs Norris instigating much of the 'evil' suffered by the other two. The trajectory of all the families is shadowed by counterfactuals that declare the power of circumstance and nurture: if Mrs Norris had had nine children she might not have become miserly and she would have been a better mother than Mrs Price; if Mrs Price had married higher she might not have been a slattern. The concluding marriage of Edmund and Fanny, two worthy children of the inadequate sisters, Lady Bertram and Mrs Price, together with the exile of Mrs Norris and her favourite niece Maria, redeems the family at considerable human expense.

The expendable Mrs Norris is, like Fanny, a dependant on the Bertrams. Like Fanny, too, she fixes affections on a single Bertram child. The similarity provokes jealousy of her niece, as does the fact that, in her fragile power, Fanny resembles her pampered sister Lady Bertram, whom Mrs Norris cannot openly resent. She is aware of the contest: when Fanny absorbs the East Room into her domain, Mrs Norris sees encroachment and orders no fire to be lit in it. The order is countermanded by a softened Sir Thomas and his act signals the decline of his sister-in-law's power. (He has yet to understand that this austere room potentially undermines his own power as thoroughly as the expensive stage erected by his disorderly children in his private library.) Mrs Norris knows who is vanquishing her: taking up again the theatrical vocabulary she sees her niece as 'the daemon of the piece'. In the end Fanny, who has liberally cried throughout the novel, sheds no tears as her aunt leaves after Maria's adultery. The now stupefied Mrs Norris has some dignity in her real affection for this privileged niece, to whom she will 'devote herself', living for the first time with someone she loves; yet the narrator acidly comments that the selfish pair will suffer 'mutual punishment'.

With a damaged legacy of women, much rests on the grave Sir Thomas, so ignorant of other people's character that he has married the most vacuous person in all of Jane Austen and so ignorant of himself that he believes good intention can make his absolute power palatable. He holds lofty notions about education but, having bought it with money, he has not involved himself in the process, except for occasional examinations. He has often been absent: beyond the sojourn in Antigua he is away each year on parliamentary business. When at home, partly through temperament, he fails in his upbringing of most of his children, including Tom, his disobliging heir, and he is almost as little loved as Mrs Norris, whose flawed surrogacy is expressed in her saving a few half crowns 'with delighted integrity' while encouraging his eldest daughter to ruin her life. Like the general in *Northanger Abbey* and indeed Darcy before Elizabeth began to tease him, Sir Thomas chills the house and makes it a prison for most of its inhabitants, repressing laughter and animation; he 'keep[s] everybody in their place' while ignorant of their inner feelings and characters. For a man so disapproving of theatricals he is much concerned with *performing* his patriarchal role. In this context his homecoming is supreme irony: he enters his 'own dear room' to find himself on a stage as the baneful *deus ex machina* of the domestic play. At the end of the novel he fears he has not encouraged 'moral principle': he never understands that his main failure has been emotional.

Sir Thomas's flaw is most evident when he lets ambition silence him over Maria, accepting like Edmund that his eldest daughter lacks strong feelings: indeed his frosty demeanour propels her into her error, for, although she marries the rich fool Rushworth in part to hide from Henry Crawford how deeply he has hurt her, how much she has trusted his histrionic gestures, she does so even more to get away from Sir Thomas: 'She was less and less able to endure the restraint which her father imposed . . . She must escape from him and Mansfield as soon as possible.' Distance has made Sir Thomas fonder of his family and he returns from Antigua intending kindness – in theory, for, when confronted with the dire realities, he falls back into his old ways. On discovering his future son-in-law a fool, he offers his daughter a release from her engagement. His kindness, however, remains 'solemn' and he is quick to accept her perfunctory assurances, feeling 'very happy' to secure an alliance 'which would bring him such an addition of respectability' (*MP*, 2:3).

Sir Thomas's fondness most attractively emerges in unexpected affection for his 'little Fanny' even before he learns of her valiant, lonely effort to uphold his rule. Like Henry Crawford's, his admiration for her new prettiness and burgeoning sexuality – marketability perhaps – embarrasses her; it indicates that men, the powerful sex and here her social superiors, will now react to her through her body. Again, however, the fondness is limited: when Fanny, given daughterly status mainly through Crawford's courtship, becomes the only child actually to oppose him, Sir Thomas reveals aspects of General Tilney in his character and he finds her opposition beyond 'comprehension'. He compounds the error he made with Maria by pushing his niece into an opportunistic match, failing to appreciate in her those principles of self-regulation he wished to instil in his daughters. In *Pride and Prejudice* Mr Bennet's marriage and resulting emotional distance from his family allowed a catastrophe similar to Sir Thomas's, but Mr Bennet learnt something from his error: even knowing his family's financial insecurity, when faced with a loved daughter's brilliant match, he advises against marriage without esteem and affection. Sir Thomas has not done better in choosing a wife and he has learnt less.

Like Mr Bennet, Sir Thomas is appalled at the sexual catastrophe in his family when he finds his daughter an adulteress. Yet, although he does not recover as speedily as Mr Bennet, he is 'not overpowered' in Edmund's words – where his deputy Mrs Norris is 'quieted, stupefied . . . benumbed'. His response is to punish Maria more than himself – in this act resembling Mr Collins as well as his brother-in-law, Mr Price, who imagines giving his niece 'the rope's end'. Accepting Mrs Norris at last as 'a part of himself', he nonetheless deflects blame on to her. It is his nemesis that by the end he welcomes what he once feared and urged Mrs Norris to make impossible – cousin marriage: he takes as daughter-in-law (Mrs Bertram), a girl he had precisely seen as not his daughter ('not a *Miss Bertram*').[5] But again change is only partial: Fanny, now the 'daughter he truly wanted', appears in transactional terms 'rich repayment' for his own 'charitable kindness', showing that his self-awareness goes only so far; he is quick to take credit for Fanny's moral integrity which he did little to encourage, yet remains reluctant to accept responsibility for his daughter's fall.

Literally or figuratively?

The earnestness of *Mansfield Park* is buttressed by a new sense of significance in its episodes, Austen's experimental use of symbolism less to structure the book than to delineate the complex interaction between inner and outer, memory and desire. Two main examples are the powerful and troubling sequence at Sotherton, named an afternoon of 'cross accidents', and the underworld episode of Fanny in Portsmouth.

During Sir Thomas's absence, encouraged by Mrs Norris, Maria enters an engagement with Mr Rushworth of Sotherton Court. The arrival at Mansfield parsonage of the vivacious Henry and Mary Crawford changes all relationships and, like the scene-painter in the theatricals who makes five of the housemaids 'dissatisfied', the pair destabilise those above stairs: both Bertram daughters are soon in love with Henry, while Edmund, the worthiest Bertram son, is captivated by Mary – though he looks grave every time she utters a sprightly riposte. His cousin Fanny, whose childish gratitude and affection are fast maturing into adult desire, looks on jealous, appalled, and mainly silent. At this point, a combined visit to Sotherton is planned, ostensibly to advise Rushworth on improving his ancient estate.

The party join together in the modernised chapel abandoned for public use by Rushworth's predecessor – with his new 'improvements' Rushworth is seeking to obliterate still more of the past. Here the social aspect of religion emerges from light chatter. The jealous sister Julia declares Maria is standing in such a way as to indicate her marriage to Rushworth. Maria's horror and Henry Crawford's flirtatious use of it – '"I do not like to see Miss Bertram so near the altar"' – clarify Maria's hopes that her engagement will be destroyed by a counter proposal. Julia also jolts the other 'courting' couple, since the wedding she imagines would be performed by Edmund, who, Mary now discovers, is destined for the Church. She is shocked, for she has mocked the 'cloth' and despises the profession: 'A clergyman is nothing.' When she remarks that the ending of private services is Sotherton's only present 'improvement' – the shy Fanny is provoked into her first long speech. She has internalised a picture of the estate reminiscent of Ben Jonson's country house poem 'To Penshurst', where 'Each morn, and even, they [the noble family] are taught to pray, / With the whole household.'[6] Her speech is a direct plea for her mentor Edmund's approval and angrily she waits for him to rebuke Mary. Instead, he later contrasts her 'lively mind' and the seriousness of the subject, stressing to Fanny the influence of environment on morals and the value of cultural restraint to police desires.

All has gone wrong in the chapel, and, as Mary remarks, people want 'air and liberty'. As soon as possible the young people exit into the pleasure grounds to find 'happy independence' and indulge in 'fault-finding', ostensibly of the estate but also of each other. They walk for a while in the wilderness – a plot of garden planted with various trees to suggest 'wild' nature but very much part of the cultivated and managed ground, a safe place especially for ladies. There Mary mischievously combats Edmund's sense of time and distance with her 'feminine lawlessness' (Fanny is 'a most accurate and honest reckoner'). Excited by her proximity he abandons his cousin for the walk and begins trying to sever his increasing desire (represented by Mary) from his reason and duty (indicated by Fanny). All except the stationary Fanny, seated because she is tired and physically weaker than the others, now stray beyond the ordered wilderness into the wilder park, anticipating their later errors of judgement and action. Mary and Edmund go through an unlocked entrance but Maria and Henry face a barrier, a locked iron gate in the ha-ha.[7]

The park beyond the wilderness draws on a long tradition of dangerous wild places, in Milton, Spenser, and Shakespeare, as well as in Richardson, where Clarissa is fooled through the gate into her seducer's power and her own ruin. In the Sotherton episode a fictional fall into too obvious symbolism is prevented by the knowingness of the actors. Without the moral fibre of the suffering Fanny, spoilt into self-satisfaction by her aunt Norris and repressed by her frosty father, Maria has for the first time felt desire and is desperate to escape Mansfield Park through Henry rather than her dull fiancé. Henry begins:

> 'You have a very smiling scene before you.'
>
> 'Do you mean literally or figuratively? Literally, I conclude. Yes, certainly, the sun shines, and the park looks very cheerful. But unluckily that iron gate, that ha-ha, give me a feeling of restraint and hardship. "I cannot get out," as the starling said.' As she spoke, and it was with expression, she walked to the gate; he followed her. 'Mr. Rushworth is so long fetching this key!'
>
> 'And for the world you would not get out without the key and without Mr. Rushworth's authority and protection, or I think you might with little difficulty pass round the edge of the gate, here, with my assistance; I think it might be done, if you really wished to be more at large, and could allow yourself to think it not prohibited.'
>
> 'Prohibited! nonsense! I certainly can get out that way, and I will. . .'
>
> (*MP*, 1:10)

Maria has moved from the Tilneys' picturesque into symbolic looking, and the literary comes to the fore. She refers to Sterne's *A Sentimental Journey* in which the hero, fearing imprisonment in France, feels kinship with a caged starling, which, however, he fails to free. The sharing of allusion allows the interchange to be part of a present playful seduction rather than simply a foreshadowing of later adultery. The poignancy of the moment is Maria's semi-awareness of what she is about, augmented by Fanny's unique effort to restrain her by warning her of physical mishap – "'You will hurt yourself.'" For, as Maria, seeing Fanny alone, knows exactly what is happening with her brother, so Fanny recognises Maria's sexual desire as she hears her speaking with Henry in such erotic code.

The Sotherton excursion ends on a quietly humorous note. With the women passengers mentally fatigued and erotically disappointed, tensions are running high in Henry's barouche: when Mrs Norris, heaving with goodies she has sponged and in customary querulous mode, demands that Fanny show gratitude for the 'indulgence' of a day out, Maria Bertram for once comes to her cousin's defence – motivated not by a sense of justice, but by her own unbounded materialism that prompts her to guard with a jealous eye even the pheasant's eggs of a man she would gladly jilt. To present with precision yet without apparent moral judgement the casual manifestations of human egotism is one of the great achievements of Austen's comedy in this novel.

Before moving to Fanny's sojourn in Portsmouth, it is worth pausing on the sequel to the Sotherton episode, the theatricals, which estrange Mansfield Park from itself by placing the ungoverned young, made unruly by the outing, in the very sanctum of the authoritarian Sir Thomas. The narrative disapproval of the project is curious to those who know that Jane Austen loved amateur theatricals and that they occurred at Steventon parsonage, especially when she was a child in the 1780s and her glamorous cousin Eliza de Feuillide was visiting. Even then, however, there was some dissent and another Austen cousin, Philadelphia, refused to act, to Eliza's amazement. By 1811 more self-restraint was being required of the gentry classes, more moral leadership of the sort Pasley required in a war-torn country suffering industrial and agricultural unrest. The melodramatic *Lovers' Vows*, not unlike the fare in the Steventon barn, is yet an unsuitable vehicle for home dramatics where there is an engaged and unprotected daughter about to face less attractive *marriage* vows.

The play was adapted from the German by Elizabeth Inchbald, whose *A Simple Story* foreshadowed some of Austen's effect in *Mansfield Park* through its contrasting heroines: flirtatious, attractive, immoral mother and modest, virtuous daughter; in struggling to win the love and esteem of her stern father, the latter points to a theme of filial–parental desire similar to that expressed in Fanny and her uncle. *Lovers' Vows* is very different: sentimentally radical in its belief in instinctive goodness, its depiction of the corrupt upper orders, acceptance of women's assertive love-making, and its assumption that fallen women can be redeemed. Where professional actors could make something of its melodramatic scenes, in a house alive with sexual frisson it must prove dangerous. Curiously, the only person who might have taken any direct moral lesson from it is Sir Thomas Bertram: in the play the patriarchal baron wrongly marries for money and years of misery ensue; he learns from his past and refuses a rich 'ape for a son-in-law', fearing his daughter would be miserable. Unfortunately, when he returns, Sir Thomas simply burns all unbound copies of the play, minimising the possibility of influence from the alien culture and assuming that his children's memory can be equally purged. Then he lets his daughter marry the 'ape' Rushworth, forcing her into action far more harmful than anything on the stage.

At Sotherton Henry and Maria had shown themselves susceptible to the freedom of symbolic acts and inevitably they use the play for erotic ends. Even Fanny most feels Henry's 'charm' when he is theatrically reading Shakespeare. Edmund, the moral deputy in Sir Thomas's absence, gives no leadership where most required: to his infatuated sisters. He abandons his principled stand against putting on the play – based on the sexist notion that, while schoolboys might declaim, '[g]rown-up daughters' should be guarded – and partners Mary as the beloved clergyman tutor to her pert pupil. Fanny, whose relationship to Edmund is actually close to the one Mary plays, alone stands firm, knowing, however, that her own shyness and jealousy of Mary form part of her repugnance. *Her* temptation comes not in the theatre but in the alternative world of Portsmouth.

The preamble to the Portsmouth episode is Henry's whim to seduce her as well as her cousins – or, as she puts it, to 'cheat her of her tranquillity', for she rightly points out to Edmund that, given her status, she could not have *expected* marriage. A vain man yet with 'moral taste' honed through life with his 'vicious' uncle, Henry can see in others what he wants for himself but will not struggle to achieve. He finds the responsive, silent, modest and devoted Fanny – he is especially attracted by her love for her brother William, which he imagines directed to himself – is just the wife he desires, the kind of woman he encouraged Maria not to be, an 'angel' and hardly a woman at all (the shallow, charming Frank Churchill will use the term for the much tormented Jane Fairfax in Austen's next novel). She will be the best of the 'improvements' he imagines for his Everingham estate. Unlike poor Mr Rushworth, however, Fanny has a retentive memory: 'The true art of memory is the art of attention', Johnson had observed in *The Idler* – a periodical stacked on her bookshelves in the East Room – and, in her usual role of watchful bystander, she had witnessed the many seduction games Henry played.[8] Thinking on these, she is appalled at Crawford's mocking reference to the 'fair bride' and declaration that he 'never was happier' when, in her terms, he was behaving 'so dishonourably and unfeelingly' (*MP*, 2:5). But, under Fanny's influence, the flexible Henry now changes roles, appealing to her by more decorous behaviour. When she refuses him, Sir Thomas weighs in, compounding his mistake with Maria, although with a difference: he accepted his daughter's marriage to a fool assuming she had no strong feelings, while now he accuses the modest Fanny of a 'heated fancy' for turning down a rich, attractive man. He refuses a fleeting glimpse of the truth, ruled out by Mrs Norris when their niece first came to Mansfield: that Fanny loves his son Edmund. Abandoning even the pretence that she has a choice, he decides to force her acceptance by sending her home to Portsmouth, where, he rightly surmises, she will get 'heartily sick' of indigence and yearn for the comforts Henry's large income can provide.

Rather like the later Emma, Fanny is a fantasist. Despite the fact that her mother readily dispatched her to richer relatives nearly a decade before, she expects to return to be first and equal in her family, long-lost daughter and visiting lady: 'To be in the centre of such a circle, loved by so many, and more loved by all than she had ever been before, to feel affection without fear or restraint' (*MP*, 3:6). Reality cannot equal this vision and she at once finds herself, like the returning Sir Thomas, 'bewildered' in her home. In disgust she turns on her disappointing mother, judged more harshly than Mary Crawford ever judges her philandering uncle, the admiral: Mrs Price is 'a dawdle, a slattern . . . who had no talent, no conversation, no affection towards herself'. (Fanny, so impressed with male authority, always tends to blame the woman rather than the man and, as the admiral's suffering wife was censured for not teaching her niece more respect for her immoral uncle, so blame here falls mainly on *Mrs* rather than *Mr* Price.) In the process Fanny even reveals jealousy of her beloved brother William: 'What right had she to be of importance to her family? She could have none, so long lost sight of! William's concerns must be dearest – they always had been – and he had every right' (*MP*, 3:7). He *does* have a right, both domestically and nationally – his ship is about to sail as part of the war fleet – but the phrase, 'they always had been', betrays Fanny's reprise of her earliest neglect.

Now, as the original dream of home collapses, she replaces it with a new fantasy: of dull and stifling Mansfield Park as what Trilling calls '"the Good place," Yeats's home "where all's accustomed, ceremonious"': a place where there is 'a consideration of times and seasons, a regulation of subject, a propriety, an attention towards every body'.[9] Although Fanny does admit 'tenderness' might be missing, the ideal still remains far from the portrait the reader has viewed. In its shadow Portsmouth becomes a kind of underworld in which

Fanny wilts: fastidiously she sends out for 'biscuits and buns' to avoid the greasily served puddings and hashes her mother provides. In this context she faces her greatest test: to accept the power and vanity of doing good, for she knows that marriage to Henry would allow her to rescue her sister Susan from this slovenly home.

The thespian Henry continues in his transformation; like the deceiving suitors of his sister's friends, he calibrates his behaviour. In Portsmouth with Fanny he becomes a watcher as she is; he is polite to and tactful with the Prices and, like Willoughby in *Sense and Sensibility*, follows the taste of the woman he pursues – the wild seascape of Portsmouth, so fashionable a topic in art, has not tempted him before and presumably will not do so again, but he appreciates it with Fanny. (Here, for once, Fanny approaches her despised father, since he has a similar aesthetic appreciation of a ship going to sea in the morning: 'perfect beauty afloat', he calls it.) For Fanny Henry employs the vocabulary of the Christian landlord – 'duty' and 'welfare' – forgetting his usual concern for self-gratifying estate 'improvement' and knowledge of 'how to turn a good income into a better'. Coupled with the influence of a comfortless home, these developments persuade Fanny that Henry himself is 'improved', although she is usually dubious about sudden alterations, either of people or landscape.

It is in part because of her sliding towards Henry in the extremity of Portsmouth that she reacts so harshly to his defection. Perhaps in retaliation for the injury she suffered, Maria ruins herself to seduce Henry and destroy his possible happiness with Fanny. He had always been aroused by Maria and, although his love for Fanny is presented as genuine – he sees her physical as well as moral beauty – he unpleasantly ties it to his fascination for Maria, once remarking of the Bertram women: 'They will now see what sort of woman it is that can attach me . . . I wish the discovery may do them any good' (*MP*, 2:12). His defection is prepared for by previous unsteadiness: he once wished to be the fighting William Price as he later wishes to have Fanny Price, but in the first case a little reflection returned him to his habitual self, the man of pleasure pleasing only himself. Frustrated by waiting too long for Fanny, Henry does not go to his neglected estate in Norfolk as suggested but to Richmond, near where Maria is staying without her husband: it is not as easy to change settled habits as didactic novelists supposed.

Henry abandons Fanny to intense and complicated feelings, for he goes as she approaches surrender. The revulsion when she hears of his betrayal is revulsion at adultery but also at herself – she sees Henry as almost engaged to her. Where Mary Crawford would downgrade infidelity and adultery to social folly, Fanny magnifies them into universal disease and chaos:

> She passed only from feelings of sickness to shudderings of horror; and from hot fits of fever to cold. The event was so shocking, that there were moments even when her heart revolted from it as impossible – when she thought it could not be. A woman married only six months ago, a man professing himself devoted, even *engaged*, to another – that other her near relation – the whole family, both families connected as they were by tie upon tie, all friends, all intimate together! – it was too horrible a confusion of guilt, too gross a complication of evil, for human nature, not in a state of utter barbarism, to be capable of!   (*MP*, 3:15)

The response underscores the excessive nature beneath Fanny's modest, restrained exterior. So explicit is her insistence on familial 'confusion' that she seems to feel that the guilty pair have committed a blood sin as well as adultery – a kind of near incest, fulfilling the narcissistic potential in familial ties which hangs over the novel: in the mother–son scenes of *Lovers' Vows*, in the initial discussion of cousin love as 'morally impossible', and in Fanny's final triumph.[10] Indeed, it seems that she herself is almost the guilty party. Yet Fanny had *not* accepted Henry: she is shuddering at the taint of being untrue to her feeling for her cousin. The passage is made the more disturbing by the narrator's earlier statement that Fanny *must* have married Henry if he had gone on – Cassandra Austen had urged her sister to make this union the ending of the book – and by the absence of any narrative comment at all close to this response; the narrator's suggestion that, if duped again, the wronged Rushworth may 'be duped at least with good humour and good luck' is worthy of Mary Crawford.

The two dearest objects on earth

In *Mansfield Park* Austen has not shifted from the concerns of the novels drafted in the 1790s, oscillation between reason and passion, and need for constant self-examination in the self's negotiation with other individuals and society. However, she has added a new national awareness of the context of such nego-tiation, a new sense of a communal social requirement to balance a burgeoning individualism. Here religion, the community of faith of the Church of England, forms part of the structure and cement of society. In a letter of 29 January 1813, Austen told her sister, 'Now I will try to write of something else; – it shall be a complete change of subject – Ordination' (*L*, p. 202). This 'change' is presum-ably in the letter rather than her novels, a letter written after *Mansfield Park* had been started, so that Austen is querying the process of clerical training. Yet, in a very broad sense, 'ordination' is a possible key to an aspect of the book which considers the value of clergymen and religion within the nation.[11]

The clerical discussion instituted by Edmund and Fanny suits the stress on work in the novel, the importance of being professional, whether in ministering, acting, or fighting – Pasley's reiterated point was that Britain needed *professional* military leadership to defeat France. Austen's novels conceived in the 1790s feature absentee, half-hearted, or ridiculous clergymen and well-dressed, leisured officers, but by the 1810s the Church and the military (equal objects of Fanny's admiration) are serious professions, linking the getting of money with morality. Yet both are ambivalently presented here: William Price is the sort of frank, thrusting, and single-mindedly ambitious young man required for combat, and, as his easy acceptance of the invitation to hunt with Henry Crawford suggests, able to move into gentlemanly ranks with ease; yet he would not have progressed without the corrupt Admiral Crawford's patronage – and perhaps a childhood under his rum-smelling father's harsh discipline. Meanwhile, the Church appears as a place of sloth and indulgence, where a man can live a gentlemanly life once he has converted his 'mere parsonage house' into a suitable residence and removed any sight of the farmland which provides a large part of his income.

Against such views Edmund expresses his serious sense of the clerical calling. Opposing the subordination of Church to social power, comically displayed when Mr Collins does Lady Catherine's bidding in *Pride and Prejudice*, he declares that a clergyman 'has the charge of all that is of the first importance to mankind, individually or collectively considered, temporally and eternally, [he] has the guardianship of religion and morals, and consequently of the manners which result from their influence' (*MP*, 1:9). Sir Thomas, who had once thought to give two livings to his son, returns from Antigua an opponent of pluralism (having more than one living – like Austen's father) and an eloquent supporter of the duties of a resident clergyman, which Edmund intends to be: 'human nature needs more lessons than a weekly sermon can convey'. In London fine preaching is a branch of acting, as Henry later suggests when he visualises himself giving an impressive sermon and receiving 'capital gratification'. But Edmund's rural parson is a model of behaviour as well as a useful preacher – like Mr Howard in *The Watsons* he will eschew 'theatrical grimace or violence' in his sermons – and an arbiter of conduct and manners. 'As the clergy are, or are not what they ought to be, so are the rest of the nation', he declares.[12]

As a result of such comments by the hero, *Mansfield Park* may seem to endorse a kind of privatisation, the idea that the public sphere can be benefited or dominated by private domestic virtues and manners. If so, it remains only a hope. Alien London with its thespian preachers and corrupt admirals exists on the edge of everyone's consciousness and is not shown as amenable to parochial influence. Domestic virtues, even of the clergy, will primarily be their own reward. Edmund Burke had written, 'Manners are of more importance than laws. Upon them, in a great measure, the laws depend . . . According to their quality, they aid morals, they supply them, or they totally destroy them.'[13] Developing this point Edmund wants to make manners into morals: 'The manners I speak of, might rather be called conduct, perhaps the result of good principles.' But his idealism is comically qualified by Susan Price's reverse reduction of manners to table habits as she travels from uncouth Portsmouth to polite Mansfield: 'Visions of good and ill breeding, of old vulgarisms and new gentilities were before her; and she was meditating much upon silver forks, napkins, and finger glasses' (*MP*, 3:15).

The discussion of the clergy raises the question of the qualities required for a clergyman's wife. Catherine Morland and Elinor Dashwood were acceptable partners for old-fashioned clergymen; Edmund's wife will have as husband a serious minister in a newly revitalised church. For this wife he has a choice between Fanny and Mary. The latter's attractions are clear, the former's less so.

Many readers have followed Henry Crawford in puzzling over Fanny: 'I do not quite know what to make of Miss Fanny. I do not understand her . . . What is her character? – Is she solemn? – Is she queer? – Is she prudish?' (*MP*, 2:6) One reply is to see her not only as a character but also as a function in a Christian context. Few would go as far as declaring her an analogy of Christ, 'a trope of redemptive good . . . in an estate and a parish that are in need of redemption', but few would deny that she is more morally serious, more insistently religious than her predecessors, more freighted with social meaning, more hungry for worlds beyond, and more closely connected with her future husband's profession.[14] Yet such characterisation does not fully comprehend her character, for Fanny is not entirely otherworldly and, although her final achievement of marriage may seem a reward, an arrangement of providence, it is not stated to be so; the narrator does not allow her to be too pious or to escape being a little ridiculous.

Her inwardness and rhapsodic response to nature, her romantic yearnings, seen in the moonlit and gothic transparencies in the East Room and in her quotations from Romantic poets, are signs of her spiritual life, a sense of 'wonder' and 'miracle'. At the same time they exaggerate the gratitude she pathetically feels at Mansfield to Edmund. The rhapsodies often mingle with erotic longing, as when she looks at Sotherton chapel through the lens of the Scott poetry she shares with Edmund or when she tries to entice him into still nature, away from the captivating, vibrating harp and human warmth of Mary Crawford in the parsonage drawing-room. In both cases Edmund dampens the rhapsodies, mentioning the late date of the building or noting Fanny's lovable 'enthusiasm'.

Her almost excessive introspection, her diffidence and inhibitions are given cause in her past, a past glimpsed through memory. She moves from home damaged and largely unloved, so becoming overconscious of her unworthiness as a poor relation as well as her need for inner self-reliance, part of the 'guide in ourselves'. *Mansfield Park* is Austen's most serious look at childhood as influence on personality and at memory as a malleable and shaping force. Fanny praises the faculty to an unresponsive Mary Crawford, herself more interested in the future than the past. She notes how memory selects outside the conscious will and yet can be adjusted to include the 'precious remains of the earliest attachments'. Where the ebullient Elizabeth Bennet had thought memory obedient and available for pleasurable selection, to Fanny the past is a restraining part of the present. When she arrives at Portsmouth, however, she finds memory erring and overwhelmed by present knowledge. As in *Pride and Prejudice*, feeling and memory can seem at odds.

Fanny and Mary are both deracinated, depending on relatives for a home; both have defensively armoured themselves, the stationary one with firm morality, the peripatetic with wit and sexy liveliness. Given her developed personality, Mary would not be a useful wife for a resident clergyman who cannot indulge in naughty jokes or see it as a 'point of honour' to promote people's enjoyment at the expense of puffing their 'vanity and pride'. Against her self-interest the competitive Mary comes to love Edmund, but, like Henry, she fantasises dominating a 'good' character: as Henry wants to 'force' Fanny to care for him, Mary imagines Edmund's 'sturdy spirit' bending towards her as 'sweet beyond expression' – her relationship, real and imagined, includes movement where Fanny's pull is towards stillness. Even when most attracted to him, however, this metropolitan woman can imagine spending only half the year in the country – and with the best society; a single wet afternoon in the Grants' parsonage bores her to distraction. All Austen novels display men whose characters have been diminished or at least not improved by injudicious marriage, Mr Allen, Mr Bennet, Mr Palmer, and Mr Elton in *Emma*. Most have followed beauty, but there may be equal error for a clergyman in marrying primarily for liveliness and erotic fascination, however attractive these qualities are to our more worldly time. (Hannah More notes 'the bewitching form of a prophane bon-mot' and the 'glitter of an epigram'.)[15] In the end, Edmund reduces what he felt for Mary to a 'charm' that can be broken.[16]

As Edmund had believed the clergyman profoundly affected the nation, so Jane West thought domestic women's moral influence could affect world affairs more 'than the wisdom of our counsellors, or the valour of our fleets and armies'.[17] Fanny cannot carry this weight; she is not exemplary, not the equivalent of Lucilla in More's didactic *Cœlebs*, whose shyness and seriousness she shares. Despite similar situations – unexpressed love and 'independence of spirit' – there is no spoken sympathy between Fanny and her female cousins: the tender heart which the narrator so often mentions is not on public display. She is quickly ashamed of her natural home and, in the talk with her uncle, lies about her main reason for rejecting Henry: love for Edmund. She spends much of the book consumed by jealousy and has a 'sore and angry' heart. She is censorious about Mary Crawford, who, on little evidence, is pronounced 'cruel' and 'ungrateful', the latter so loaded a word in Fanny's lexicon that her judgement appears warped by her own experience. Like Maria and Julia with Henry, she tries to conquer her passion for Edmund: she has more reason since it seems to her a taboo, although a social rather than biological one, a love that should not even speak its name: 'Why did such an idea occur to her even enough to be reprobated and forbidden? It ought not to have touched on the confines of her imagination.' Here her usual obedience to 'ought' fails and, as in her response to Henry's defection, the reader is given a glimpse of implied depths of desire.

Yet, Fanny remains more suited to a clerical life in the country than the vibrant Mary. She is in training for goodness, examining herself and repeatedly struggling against wayward impulses and poor health. Although Trilling referred to it as 'alienating', the weakness is a given rather than a fault and the reader is reprimanded for a tendency to follow the Bertram sisters in seeing robustness as a virtue.[18] Fanny has known neglect, but Edmund's responsive kindness has made 'tears delightful' and turned homesickness into love, so that she learns to assimilate pain into her personality. With her seriousness, her active sense of duty and keen sense of the power of self-restraint and -denial, then, she would make a good rural clergyman's wife: with her Edmund's profession would become a common pursuit. He requires such a wife since, although he reverts to being 'every thing good and great', he has erred in his first romantic choice and compromised his profession. Tactfully Fanny does not allude to his blindness to her emotions and appalling collusion in the family efforts to force her into a loveless match, made the more reprehensible by his selfish motive: his belief that a marriage between his cousin and Henry Crawford would further his own chances with Mary.

Part of the complexity of Fanny's presentation and struggle with Mary Crawford is the narrative voice, more slippery in this book than in any other: more committed at one moment, more distant at another, sometimes seemingly at one with 'my' Fanny's subjectivity, especially in the second half, at others ironically detached or entering another consciousness. Occasionally the voice is morally definite, at others unexpectedly arch. With all the earnestness of debate, there is yet more emphasis here than in *Pride and Prejudice* on the story as fiction, and the tone of the last pages, reminiscent of the playful close of *Northanger Abbey*, is light, rounding off an often grim story with flippancy and a metafictional insistence on fictionality. 'Other pens' are left to dwell on 'guilt and misery' while the reader is entreated to hold to a vision of life as comedy, rather at odds with most of the book. The only other Austen novel of similar bleakness, *Sense and Sensibility*, shrugs into the final union of Marianne and Colonel Brandon with a question: 'What could she do?' Here, too, the narrator asks, 'What could be more natural than the change?' as Edmund, deeply in love with another and vibrant woman throughout most of the novel, almost to the last pages, moves into being gratefully and 'naturally' in love with the still Fanny, as if it were a seasonal matter, sighing 'with *you*, Fanny, there may be peace'. Here it is possible to sympathise with Marvin Mudrick's view that irony is 'Jane Austen's defense against feeling'.

Yet, the novel encloses feeling, even passion, to an extraordinary degree, and, as so often, it is not the less intense for being one-sided. Concentrating on the physical body of this least robust of Austen heroines, John Wiltshire argues that the inhibited Fanny, the 'still, principled, fulcrum of moral right' should be 'understood as a trembling, unstable entity . . . erotically driven and conflicted'.[19] In *Mansfield Park* there is none of the flirtatious sparring Elizabeth and Darcy so enjoyed; in its place are freighted conversations of chiming or dissonant, sometimes half-conscious, desires, with raw emotions beneath the surface of words.

See, for example, the scene where Edmund, having decided to give in to the theatricals and act after all, comes to Fanny in her liminal East Room, surrounded by the signs of her own particular culture, her reading and her pictures. She is contemplating her refusal to act, worrying whether it is through shyness rather than principle and whether she is being ungrateful to her cousin Tom, the prime mover of the play. All the way through the book she has wrestled with the idea of gratitude – which Mrs Norris imposed on her as a frightened child of ten arriving at the Park. Now she worries how much she owes to others. She looks at Tom's gifts and 'grew bewildered as to the amount of the debt' – what does 'duty' say she owes? At this moment, when she is mentally testing herself and her motives, Edmund enters, 'before whom all her doubts were wont to be laid'.

He has come not to resolve hers but to allay his own. He is trying to unite his two beloved women by endowing Mary with Fanny's qualities. Having worried about her own impure motives, Fanny sees *his* impurity: Edmund's passion has misled his judgement – he wants to act so as to prevent Mary's intimacy with another man, not simply to keep the theatricals private. Fanny understands his self-deceiving manoeuvre since she herself uses it – at Portsmouth when she ascribes anger at the treatment of herself to disrespect for Mansfield Park, or when she hides jealousy of Mary under pity for a horse ridden too vigorously.

Edmund's strategy silences her at first, since she can neither applaud, her usual role, nor criticise. When she rallies, he cuts her short, discerning his own semi-dishonesty; yet he then pleads his case in terms that reveal his love for Mary and blindness to Fanny's feelings: 'Put yourself in Miss Crawford's place.' The demand stings Fanny and for the first time she criticises Edmund directly: 'I am sorry for Miss Crawford; but I am more sorry to see you drawn in to do what you had resolved against.' She is revealing a new maturity by precisely not seeing everything as Edmund sees it – her earlier stance. (Similarly, despite reverence for Sir Thomas's opinions, she 'come[s] out' as an adult when, desperate not to appear 'ungrateful', she can yet conclude, 'romantic delicacy' could not be expected from a man 'who had married a daughter to Mr Rushworth'.) Here, strenuously trying to be the domestic conduct-book ideal, Fanny is perilously close to infringing the demand that a woman not try to control a man's conduct. Her unease, coupled with her jealousy, results in mean-spiritedness, and she adds: 'It will be such a triumph to the others!'

This response allows Edmund to rally against her, but he remains anxious, noting Fanny is not won over. In the end he abandons argument and appeals emotionally: 'Give me your approbation, then, Fanny, I am not comfortable without it.' The fraternal declaration overwhelms Fanny, who can only exclaim 'Oh, cousin!' It is not enough and Edmund almost accuses her of what he half glimpses, her jealousy: 'I thought *you* would have entered more into Miss Crawford's feeling.' Seeing her mistake, Fanny tries 'for greater warmth of manner' but, as she begins to fall into her usual role of pleasing Edmund, her 'conscience' stops her, that is, her consciousness of what she feels. Now Edmund refuses to interpret her silence correctly and he leaves satisfied, denying what he had glimpsed both about himself and his cousin, whom he reinstates as spinsterly, solitary reader in her bookish 'little establishment'. Blindly he remarks, 'as soon as I am gone, you will empty your head of all this nonsense of acting, and sit comfortably down to your table'. Left alone and fully accepting her own passion, Fanny finds that jealousy has effaced anxiety about her own conduct: 'She cared not how it ended . . . it was all misery *now*' (*MP*, 1:16).[20]

On a first reading of *Mansfield Park*, romance seems subdued. The love that should have been Maria's is refused; Henry's is given to Fanny, who does not want it; Fanny gets a forlorn Edmund at the expense of almost everyone else, having survived the conventional fictional 'fever' – a sleepless night of agony. But this is not the only impression of the novel. If we turn back to Fanny's extreme physical answer to Maria's and Henry's adultery, then go forwards a very short time to Edmund's report of Mary Crawford's inadequate response – she showed 'no reluctance, no horror, no feminine . . . no modest loathings' – we find Fanny contemplating everyone's miseries and feeling 'she was, in the greatest danger of being exquisitely happy': like the later exemplary Anne Elliot, she revels in the moment when her rival's moral inferiority finally becomes apparent to the hero. This response is very different from the John- sonian sounding 'consciousness of being born to struggle and endure', which the contrite Sir Thomas takes as her exemplary message. Rather, it displays 'the enthusiasm of a woman's love', in keeping with the secret fetishising of the scrap of Edmund's letter bearing the conventional 'My very dear Fanny'. The early critic Richard Whately wrote of '[t]he silence in which this passion is cherished – the slender hopes and enjoyments by which it is fed – the restlessness and jealousy with which it fills a mind naturally active, contented and unsuspicious – the manner in which it tinges every event and every reflection'.[21] The men, Edmund and Henry, abandon their love when they find obstacles – Fanny retains her hungry love whatever seems in its way.

Chapter 7

Emma

Emma is the most intricate, stylish, and elegant of Jane Austen's novels.[1] Through a concentration on the perspective of the heroine, through internal monologue, and through the most complex use of free indirect speech, the reader is forced to identify with a character displaying Lydia Bennet's 'hurtful degree of self-consequence'; Austen wrote that Emma is a heroine 'no one but myself will much like' (*Memoir*, p. 119).[2] Unlike the heroines that precede and follow her, she is little occupied with her motives and memory or with past events; being a plotter, she naturally looks to a future she expects to control – as it turns out, a futile endeavour, frequently hurtful to the unwitting pawns in her fantasy dramas. That the overall effect of the book is comic rather than cruel is due in part to the narrative techniques and in part to the sheer linguistic vitality of the fictive world, coupled with the attractive energy of the heroine. It is as if Jane Austen, having just insisted on her readers' appreciation of the weak, inhibited Fanny Price, dares us to accept a rescue of Mary Crawford, another woman with a 'lively mind' and a desire to act with something of a man's freedom, and to see in her a resemblance to the approved Elizabeth Bennet after all. The title page reads 'by the author of "Pride and Prejudice"', not *Mansfield Park*, the previous novel.

What struck the earliest readers of *Emma* was less its vitality than its lack of story. Disloyally, John Murray remarked that it wanted 'incident and Romance', and Maria Edgeworth, to whom Austen had sent a complimentary copy, read only the first volume and commented,

> there was no story in it, except that Miss Emma found that the man whom she designed for Harriet's lover was an admirer of her own – & he was affronted at being refused by Emma & Harriet wore the willow – and *smooth, thin water-gruel* is according to Emma's father's opinion a very good thing & it is very difficult to make a cook understand what you mean by *smooth, thin water-gruel*!! (*FR*, p. 231)

To Edgeworth this lack of surface story was a failing, to Austen its strength. In 1801 she wrote to Cassandra that her 'Adventures' since the last letter 'have not been very numerous': she has been to church twice, attempted a walk and found it too cold, inspected a house to let but found that it would not do, and been present at a sparsely attended ball (*L*, pp. 84–5). In the letter and the novel, the wry effect is gained by the implied comparison with usual fictional 'Adventures'.[3] Emma's most dramatic moment is Mr Elton's proposal in a coach, embarrassing and indeed painful given the implications for Harriet's potentially ruined life, but low-keyed in comparison with the numerous and violent coach episodes in novels from Richardson to Burney and beyond.

The lack of story is in part the subject of *Emma*, as it is of the letter: life's tedium and how to make it bearable. Consider the famous passage where the heroine stands at Ford's shop door waiting for her friend to complete her purchases:

> Much could not be hoped from the traffic of even the busiest part of Highbury; – Mr. Perry walking hastily by, Mr. William Cox letting himself in at the office door, Mr. Cole's carriage horses returning from exercise, or a stray letter-boy on an obstinate mule, were the liveliest objects she could presume to expect; and when her eyes fell only on the butcher with his tray, a tidy old woman travelling homewards from shop with her full basket, two curs quarrelling over a dirty bone, and a string of dawdling children round the baker's little bow-window eyeing the gingerbread, she knew she had no reason to complain, and was amused enough; quite enough still to stand at the door. A mind lively and at ease, can do with seeing nothing, and can see nothing that does not answer.   (*E*, 2:9)

In this book 'nothing' aims to 'answer'. It has to – for there is nothing more necessary or cheerful than to see the world realistically but with enough imaginative power to let it 'answer'. The book reveals the desirability – and difficulty – of holding the two ways of seeing in balance. 'Some desire is necessary to keep life in motion, and he, whose real wants are supplied, must admit those of fancy', wrote Samuel Johnson.[4] This emotional and social economy is played out in the village society of Highbury rather than in the single house of Mansfield Park or in a single individual.

Happy and rich

Cheerfulness allows comfort and ease in mundane life; it is related but not identical to 'happiness' and to the conduct-book requirement of gratitude for what one has. The bluestocking Catherine Talbot called it '*Accommodableness*':

'Every Thing is beautiful in its Season. All we have to do, is to open our Minds to so rich a Variety of delightful Impressions: to accommodate ourselves with Joy and Thankfulness to the present Scene, whatever it is.'[5] Emma's cheerful disposition allows pleasure in what might seem restricted and dull; it lets her get through with tolerable ease what might otherwise be insufficient.

Yet this cheerfulness is ambiguous and may mask inadequacy. Emma's friend Mr Weston is cheerful, but not especially deep in his feeling; John Knightley, her brother-in-law, rightly judges him more sociable than familial – he remarries only when economically ready and equably waits years to see his only son. The spinster Miss Bates seems cheerful and silly, and she infuriates Emma throughout the novel. 'Happiness' may be even more suspect; Emma's young companion Harriet Smith protests she is 'happy' when most conflicted: 'Nobody cares for a letter', she says while trying to suppress her obvious affection for its writer Robert Martin, 'the thing is, to be always happy with pleasant companions' (*E*, 1:7). When Emma works to destroy Martin's powerful effect, she makes Harriet exclaim: 'I am never happy but at Hartfield.' A claim of happiness may be defence against pain and disappointment.

Certainly it masks Emma's social isolation, an isolation which partly comes from her desire for pre-eminence; in his 1816 review Walter Scott called Emma 'the princess paramount'. Although narratively introduced as 'happy', self-satisfied, and rich, with choices no other Austen heroine possesses, the first time the reader hears from her directly she is in danger of suffering 'intellectual solitude'. Her home village of Highbury, whose 'brilliant days' have passed, contrasts with Mansfield in remoter rural Northamptonshire; from Mansfield London appeared distant and decadent, but Highbury is so close it almost feels the metropolitan tentacles of a city that has by now passed its million and which provides it with consumer goods like pianos, picture frames, and folding screens and services like hairdressing and dentistry. The village is both declining and modernising: its ballroom at the main inn is used only for a whist club, but it has added a post office and a successful bourgeoisie in Messrs Perry, Cox, and Cole, doctor, lawyer, and merchant, whose rise mirrors the decline of the clerisy, the Bateses, and their old parish clerk. (Even in *Mansfield Park* the financial drawbacks of the Church without old-fashioned patronage and fortune were accepted). Emma wants Highbury to remain almost feudal, stationary through time, so that she will always be 'paramount'. Like her tremulous father, as indolent as Lady Bertram but more dominating, she is represented as fearing uncontrollable change or any disturbance of the social scene that privileges and constrains her. She worries that after a dance people will have difficulty 'returning into their proper place'. Hence she must keep herself apart from the most enterprising sections of her community.

Jane Austen subtly portrays Emma's horror of social encroachment by showing how it blinkers her and associates her with those she most despises. Through
this portrayal we are invited not just to mock absurd characters, as Emma tries
to do, but to see their resemblance to those with whom we identify. In the carriage when the vicar Mr Elton proposes, the event is delivered solely through
Emma's eyes, which see not a sexual but a social assault. Emma is as culpable as
Mr Elton: he is shocked at her assumption that he would accept the illegitimate
Harriet Smith as his wife, and she is appalled that he considers himself her
equal. Her horror suggests some social instability, similar to that displayed by
Mr Elton's next choice: Augusta Hawkins, who relates to Emma much as the
cunning Lucy Steele did to Elinor in *Sense and Sensibility*. Both Emma and
Mrs Elton are conceited about their 'independent resources' while displaying
little of them; both have been the object of Mr Elton's pursuit; later both want
to manipulate the squire, Mr Knightley – Mrs Elton requires him to be more
familiar, Emma more distant – and both have rather unclear class status: Mrs
Elton has an uncle 'in the law line' and Emma her remote noble antecedents.[6]

Emma and Mrs Elton belittle those below them. Mrs Elton condescends
to the refined Jane Fairfax, while Emma, empathetic with the very poor –
she 'could allow for their ignorance and their temptations, had no romantic
expectations of extraordinary virtue from those, for whom education had done
so little' – is insensitive about those closer to her level. 'One should be sorry to
see greater pride or refinement in the teacher of a school' (*E*, 1:7), she remarks,
and she seeks opportunities to snub the modest but rising Coles. She sees
Harriet's lover Robert Martin not as an up-and-coming farmer who writes and
expresses himself well, but as a clownish yeoman of feudal times, although she
observes that his sisters have had 'a superior education'. Curiously, she declares
that Martin cannot become 'rich through speculation' – possibly the ultimate
source of her own wealth – when no one beside herself considers the possibility.
In this need to *degrade* there appears a faint fear of others' degrading her. To
Harriet, who, she considers, must be 'a gentleman's daughter' because she is
pretty, well-mannered, and respectful of Emma and her father, she remarks,
there 'will be plenty of people who would take pleasure in degrading you'.

As this remark suggests, Emma is often opaque and there are hints in her
of impulses never quite explored, encouraging the reader to speculate on what
may be hidden. For all the energetic confidence of her speech and displayed
thoughts, she often provides a failed example of Adam Smith's ideal 'impartial
spectator', described in his *Theory of Moral Sentiments*. Instead of judging
others through reference to her own emotions, then seeing herself through the
presumed eyes of an impartial spectator, as Smith proposes, Emma imposes
her own ideas and obscure fears on others. Having played adored wife – or

rather husband – to her weak and coercive father since her mother's early death, she has come to assume that she lacks the qualities more virile men want. It is reasonable to suppose that her sister had startled her adolescence by being chosen by Mr Knightley's clever brother John. Along with the fecund, sweet, and limited Isabella and the obliging governess, the simple Harriet (all one-time inhabitants of Hartfield under Emma), seems what men desire: 'I know that such a girl as Harriet is exactly what every man delights in – what at once bewitches his senses and satisfies his judgment', she tells George Knightley (*E*, 1:8). As a result of this emotional fear and her lively mind, Emma uses other women as substitutes for her guarded self – very unlike Marianne in *Sense and Sensibility*, whom she otherwise resembles in the making of romance in life. So she acts through them in the heterosexual, adult world of love and marriage, while at the same time usurping the freedom of a man or parent in relation to them. She becomes an 'imaginist', both a substitute author and a reader, using real-life characters for her own emotional needs.

Something her home required

The governess, now Mrs Weston, was supposed to have replaced Emma's clever mother, but instead became a replacement sister, joining the circle of admiration that Mr Woodhouse makes round his remaining daughter. Although Emma obscures the fact, Mrs Weston knows she was no equal: the fierce remarks of Jane Fairfax about the status of governesses underline this and the ex-governess seems to accept it when she comments on Jane's engagement to her rich stepson Frank, 'it is not a connexion to gratify'. Presumably this compliments her own choice, Emma, but it also suggests assimilation of Emma's own oppressive social values, since her stepson is marrying on the same level as his father. Mr Knightley, too, points out that the relationship of Emma and Mrs Weston has been unequal: for him the governess has acted less as Emma's sister than as her servile wife.

With such 'parents', Emma has not had to outgrow her favoured child status at Hartfield nor enter the adult world of marriage and adult emotion. As the ignored reading lists and excessive self-confidence of her pupil attest, Mrs Weston has been a flawed tutor; she also fails the grown-up Emma when she encourages her potentially harmful belief in the attraction of her stepson Frank and, far more, in letting Emma selfishly patronise Harriet, where the prime danger is to the unprotected girl. The main hazard for the heroine is defection; although Emma accepts her governess's marriage by persuading herself she made it, in a later scene she sees that her own engagement to Mr Knightley pleases but does not consume Mrs Weston: 'If any thing could increase her delight, it was perceiving that the baby would soon have outgrown its first set of caps.'

The paid governess as friend is succeeded by another quasi-companion, the younger, sillier, and more grateful Harriet Smith, comically reprising Fanny Price in her translation to the great house through a powerful patron. This time Emma is clearly presented as using another for self-gratification: Harriet is 'not inconveniently shy' and has 'proper and becoming' deference – she calls Emma 'Miss Woodhouse' throughout. Harriet is 'exactly the something which her home required', the sentimental friend she has read about in novels. With Harriet, Emma can make plots in the manner John and Isabella Thorpe had done for Catherine in *Northanger Abbey*. She is aware of her authorial role: in the managed courtship scene of Mr Elton and Harriet, Emma refers both to a prologue and to a mode change from poetry to prose.

Rather like the monster in *Frankenstein*, Mary Shelley's youthful novel written in the year of *Emma*'s publication, the ladylike Harriet is a product of social isolation. Although Emma – and indeed Mrs Weston – insists on using the gentler word 'blunder', there is real potential 'evil' in the 'unnatural' tie between the two young women. Presumptuously Emma assumes knowledge of Harriet's inner feelings – they were not 'of that superior sort', not 'acute and retentive' – and she imposes on Harriet her own grave social error; because she has played the husband in her home since the age of twelve, she believes she can cross gender and confer status: 'What! think a farmer, (and with all his sense and all his merit Mr. Martin is nothing more,) a good match for my intimate friend!' (*E*, 1:8). Marvin Mudrick first stressed the fascination and inadmissible homoerotic love Emma felt for the pretty Harriet, whom only she and Robert Martin ever really admire.[7] At times the relationship sounds marital: Emma reflects, 'I would not change you for the clearest-headed, longest-sighted, best-judging female breathing' (*E*, 2:13). Like the ideal wife, Harriet never takes attention from Emma: when she falls ill at Hartfield, she is eager to be gone to her motherly headmistress and cause no trouble to her friend. Emma demands absolute affection, pitting herself against the lover, until she forces Harriet to declare: 'I would not give up the pleasure and honour of being intimate with you for any thing in the world' (*E*, 1:7). She has made Harriet choose her over a man and become dependent on her, the fate which, according to Mr Knightley, Mrs Weston happily avoided.

Emma chooses for Harriet a suitor who will allow her own 'intimacy' to last 'forever': the pragmatic Mr Elton, who is to defeat the passionate farmer Robert Martin. She then tries to overpower Harriet with her visions, picturing Mr Elton in London thinking of his beloved – she even gives him a loving family ready to receive his illegitimate bride: 'how busy their imaginations all are!' But Harriet, a giggling boarding-school child of seventeen, still growing, is not entirely controlled and is not quite the simpleton Emma assumes. At times she resists. Concerned always to be the controlling watcher, never the object of others' gaze, Emma is surprised when Harriet turns the gaze on her, insisting on seeing her benefactor as a potential 'old maid', like Miss Bates. Emma responds with curious rhetoric:

> I am sure I should be a fool to change such a situation as mine. Fortune I do not want; employment I do not want; consequence I do not want: I believe few married women are half as much mistress of their husband's house, as I am of Hartfield; and never, never could I expect to be so truly beloved and important; so always first and always right in any man's eyes as I am in my father's.   (*E*, 1:10)

She claims she likes being an aunt because a mother's love is blind and warm and she wishes to see clearly and coldly. Yet Harriet continues to assert the reality of the spinsterhood embodied in Miss Bates. Perhaps this is because she herself has inspired the sexual love in Martin so obviously missing from Emma's declaration and presumed to be absent from Miss Bates's narrowed and (to Emma) threatening life. It is a clever move, for Emma is obsessed with the horror of Miss Bates.

By the end of the novel, Harriet is even more self-confident. She had always partly escaped Emma, as revealed in the disjointed speech which greets the instruction to aim at Mr Elton and forget Robert Martin:

> I shall always feel much obliged to him, and have a great regard for – but that is quite a different thing from – and you know, though he may like me, it does not follow that I should – and certainly I must confess that since my visiting here I have seen people –.   (*E*, 1:7)

But, when her mentor has failed in her schemes, Harriet, once a 'humble, grateful, little girl', can exclaim concerning the mistake over Mr Knightley as her next supposed lover: 'Oh! Miss Woodhouse, how you do forget!' Harriet is growing up, but Emma sees in this transformation only her own handiwork. Like her father, she has trouble accepting the existence of people she cannot control. Perhaps this is why, when Mr Knightley proposes, she feels such exultation in her triumph over Harriet: despite the 'serious' nature of the situation, like Elizabeth Bennet before her Emma 'must laugh'. The heroine's laughter and Austen's breezy narration swiftly move towards a 'comedy of errors' ending, in which Harriet's tooth breaks rather than her heart.

The friend Emma should have had is Miss Bates's niece Jane Fairfax, her superior in abilities but not wealth, brought up, unlike Emma, by 'right-minded and well-informed people'. Because the novel sees so much only through Emma's eyes, it is some time before the reader notices in the reserved Jane a troubled woman, heir of Fanny Price in nervous suffering. Emma ascribes her dislike to this reserve, later explained by the hidden engagement, but it began long before as jealousy, for Emma had been 'depreciating' her for the two years of their separation. When she sees her again, she is struck by Jane's appearance: elegant, tall, graceful, and 'blooming', with the height, the 'dark eyelashes and eye-brows' Emma had wrongly given Harriet when she drew her for Mr Elton. The 'bloom' is of someone beloved and admired, and the reserve is of a bespoken woman in a social world in which marriage must take precedence over all other ties: Jane is paying the price of an adulthood that Emma has not achieved with her schoolgirlish desire for 'intimacy' with Harriet.

Given her orphaned state and beauty, Jane seems marked for a heroine of romance. When not actually conversing with her, Emma, clearly a great novel reader herself, notes this aspect.[8] Yet she does not follow up Mr Knightley's suggestion that some understanding exists between her and the eligible Frank, although the secret engagement is crucial to many popular novels, such as Burney's *Cecilia*. Emma is less engrossed by memory than Fanny Price and consequently fails to read the signs given consciously and unconsciously by Frank Churchill. Instead, she insists on putting Jane into a drama of intrigue, giving her a discreditable adulterous love for her pseudo-sister's husband. This relationship follows that between Emma and her brother-in-law John Knightley, reinforcing the notion that his choice of Isabella had been a defining moment in Emma's emotional maturation. When she learns the truth, Emma recasts Jane in gothic mode: her actions to Jane have been villainy, the airing in the Hartfield carriage 'the rack', and the gift of arrow-root 'poison'. Emma comes close to Jane only when she starts using imagination to understand rather than impose: on learning of the engagement she calls it 'a system of hypocrisy and deceit – espionage, and treachery' but, almost immediately after, admits, 'If a woman can ever be excused for thinking only of herself, it is in a situation like Jane Fairfax's.' The new understanding is at Harriet's expense: 'Birth, abilities, and education, had been equally marking one as an associate for her, to be received with gratitude; and the other – what was she?' (*E*, 3:12).

Although Emma may warm to Jane Fairfax, she does not do so to her aunt. Unlike Elinor Dashwood with the good-hearted, garrulous Mrs Jennings, Emma never loses her resentment of the talkative Miss Bates. The parallel of herself and Miss Bates proposed by Harriet was rejected, but Emma is haunted by another closer one: between Miss Bates and her father. Like Mrs Churchill with Frank, Mr Woodhouse and Miss Bates are presented as lovingly coercive and suffocating parental figures. Emma pities Jane her imprisonment with her aunt, and Mr Perry ascribes her illness in part to her claustrophobic circumstances. But Emma's own servitude to an exacting father, obsessed with controlling everyone's intake of food, neither results in self-pity nor in pity from the apothecary.

Catherine Morland and Emma are the only Austen heroines not ashamed of their relatives. Throughout the book Emma is seen anticipating her father's feeble wants and manipulating him into ease.[9] One might argue that her fear of change derives from the extraordinary life this selfish, adoring man has created for her. His source of income is never declared, but presumably he has a fortune in public funds or government stock. In his 1807 treatise on nervous diseases, Thomas Trotter associated 'sloth and inactivity' with 'easy fortune', claiming that 'The public funds of this country are one great cause of those torpid habits of living; where the security of property is so compleat, that any care about its safety is needless.'[10] Rich Mr Woodhouse has no landlord duties; he owns a few pigs and poultry for domestic use and has pretty ornamental rather than functional grounds.

In his torpor, he fears movement and any external events: the departure of a daughter or a governess, the approach of gypsies, even an outing in his own coach. He diminishes everything round him. The half-glass of wine offered to Mrs Goddard becomes a small half and is then diluted with water. Similarly, he contracts Emma's world – even appealing to his coachman's needs when her interests conflict with his own – until she is almost housebound: she has never been to the sea, may not even have gone to London, cannot walk the half-mile to Randalls on her own (in striking contrast to Elizabeth Bennet and, indeed, Jane Fairfax, who walks from Donwell to Highbury alone, to Emma's amazement), and has not visited Donwell for two years. As a result she is more restricted than Fanny Price, yet less aware of it. Mrs Weston notes the absence of friends, and Mr Knightley of potential suitors. That Mr Woodhouse's 'gentle selfishness' has less dire results than the authoritarianism of Sir Thomas in *Mansfield Park* suggests that, as Emma herself surmises when considering the spoiling of Mrs Weston's baby daughter, unwise adoration is less damaging than wiser tyranny, and some self-consequence is not entirely a bad thing for a woman. Nonetheless, Mr Woodhouse's defective parenting has made his clever daughter live in a cocoon and fear the unruly world outside.

This is why she reacts so badly to an event away from Hartfield: the outing to Box Hill, not part of her usual 'feudal' scene but a rural place designed simply for modern tourist pleasure which exerts no power of 'union' over its visitors. (Gilpin saw a kind of foreignness about the place, noting 'The whole scene makes a good Alpine picture.')[11] There characters become most out of control, Miss Bates too garrulous, the Eltons too rude, Frank too subversive, and Emma too frank. She fails to realise that the public role of sardonic commentator, taken sometimes by the antisocial John Knightley, is not open to a lady and for a moment she fractures her community with her wit.[12] When, in a verbal game, Miss Bates offers to say 'three things very dull indeed', it might have been on the tip of many tongues to reply, but only Emma 'could not resist' retorting, 'Pardon me – but you will be limited as to number – only three at once.' In *Pride and Prejudice* Darcy has to learn to curb his tongue after he delivers his gratuitous insult to Elizabeth Bennet at a provincial ball. Here the insult halts Miss Bates as she instantly comprehends Emma's hurtful meaning: 'I must make myself very disagreeable, or she would not have said such a thing to an old friend' (*E*, 3:7). The nastiness of Emma's retort is underlined by its juxtaposition with the less obvious cruelty of the outsider Frank Churchill, whose barbed remarks about ill-conceived and hasty marriages Jane receives as body blows while watching his public flirting with Emma.

In her letters, Jane Austen gives little quarter to Miss Bates's real-life equivalents. She was irritated by the vacuous Mrs Digweed's distracted speech (Mrs Digweed retaliated by declaring that, had she not known the author, she 'could hardly have got through' *Emma*, *FR*, p. 231). Some critics feel similarly about the fictional character: one makes dislike of her 'relentless, tedious chirping' a touchstone of taste, maintaining that many readers skip her 'stupefying wash of gossip, triviality, and inanity'. In this reading, Emma's retort becomes equivalent to our own 'escapes and exits'.[13] What this approach ignores, however, is that Miss Bates is the quintessence of the Austenian comic character: much of the humour in her fiction grows from the unchecked natter of one-track minds who, oblivious to their surroundings, reveal their absurd obsessions and selfish motives. And *Emma*, more than any other novel, allows the brainless to babble on without restraint: Mr Woodhouse and his desire for halting and shutting out life, Mrs Elton and her need to see her expedient marriage as fairy-tale romance.

Another bleaker view is that Miss Bates conveys an 'existential loneliness', disclosing 'the possibility of an "inner" life omitted in the story proper'.[14] There is some truth to this. Her cheerfulness is overly resolute and does have a disturbing quality: old, poor, and lacking any entertaining cultural resources, she yet must please and be pleased if she is to flourish, and gratitude has to be her mode; so her stuttering, tedious speech may sometimes suggest the choking of repressed feelings. Perhaps, though, the latter view is too close to Emma's appreciation of Jane Fairfax only when she makes her into a romantically pathetic governess.

Emma never gives up her contempt for the older spinster. She never engages with her, despite at one point perceiving that she expresses the vulnerable condition of all women. Yet Miss Bates has a pivotal role in the novel's affective social theme. She is necessary to the community and its 'cheerfulness', and an insult to her becomes a general insult. Her persistent talk is inclusive; greeting all, she is at the hub of exchanges on ailments and the weather, as well as the physical exchange of food: pork and broth from Hartfield, apples from Donwell, baked in the Wallises' oven (only her niece Jane interrupts this circulation by refusing Emma's gift of arrowroot). Emma and Frank rupture the outing to Box Hill and, despite Mr Knightley's best intentions, the strawberry-picking at Donwell is not enjoyable, but at the Crown Inn ball, contrived by Frank but nearly spoilt by his irritation with Mrs Elton, Miss Bates provides almost euphoric cohesion with her gathering talk. On that occasion, after being forgotten, she and Jane are fetched in the Eltons' carriage. Miss Bates arrives and in her gushing speech transforms the dingy room into 'fairy-land'. Later, retaining her sense of painful reality, she leaves alone on foot to put her old mother to bed, then quietly returns. In striking contrast to the images of her created by both Emma and Mr Knightley, she remarks: 'I am not helpless.'

Miss Bates understands her place but is not over-deferential, so she can bind together disparate elements – it is significant that the impudent Wallises are polite only to her. More than anyone else, she holds the village's communal memory: she remembers the good orchard, old John as a young clerk, and Emma as an infant. With the boring Miss Bates, the reader may see that community has to be created and recreated through social habit or sociability by all its members, and that only by such means are poverty and lowly status made bearable – for not everyone can, with Emma, command 'the best treatment'. Such social inclusiveness helps make a bulwark against real evil: supported by a good man and prying, worthy neighbours, susceptible Harriet will not, like Maria Bertram, be 'led into temptation', assumed possible without these aids (young women are especially vulnerable in *Emma*). Perhaps it is as well for Miss Bates's efforts that her niece and Frank leave the village at the end, for Jane with her melodramatic flair and Frank with his enjoyment of subterfuge had better continue their story somewhere else.

Concealing a deeper game

As consideration of Miss Bates suggests, *Emma* is about different ways of looking and speaking, continuing here the investigation throughout the novels, but especially clear in *Pride and Prejudice*. An early conversation finds one person seeing the weather as glum and damp, another as fresh and invigorating; in Donwell, one finds the sun bright and not oppressive, another glaring. The work is full of deceptions and comic misinterpretations. More clearly than in earlier novels, here language is a game, a tool for manipulating the naïve and trusting. The point is mirrored in the playfulness of the narrative and the narrator's language, which simply deceive the first-time reader. Within the story, charades are clearly treacherous but all words have similar slippery potential, and riddling is only an extreme version of the entire book and much of its dialogue.

Emma delights in conundrums. The uninterpreted 'Kitty, a fair but frozen maid' is a bawdy riddle chosen, teasingly for the reader, by the impotent Mr Woodhouse, who fails to get past the first stanza or see he has rendered his own daughter close to being 'fair but frozen'. Mr Elton's courtship riddle is guessed wrongly by Harriet, rightly by Emma, though she misinterprets its purpose. In *Northanger Abbey*, gothic romance filled and fuddled the mind, while poetry was reduced to mnemonic phrases to grace the accomplished girl; here prose fiction and drama hold sway, while poetry, so potent for Fanny Price in *Mansfield Park* (and Anne Elliot in *Persuasion*), is reduced to puzzles.

In the main social mystery, Frank and Jane's 'deeper game', Mr Knightley becomes the detective to Frank's trickster criminal, a role far clearer on second reading. In the alphabet game at Hartfield, Harriet gets the word 'blunder' but cannot interpret it, while Mr Knightley, seeing subterfuge, remains puzzled. The game is, in fact, not a contest but a covert message to Jane from Frank, who has almost revealed their secret correspondence by appearing to know what his stepmother had not told him: that the apothecary Mr Perry planned to set up a carriage. Jane and Emma observe the name 'Dixon' but read it differently: Emma sees a non-existent intrigue, Jane a hurtful surmise in which Emma and Frank are colluding. Emma catches the same intrigue when Frank anonymously sends a piano from the affluent world of London to the poor Bates home, giving Jane a significance as exciting as improper. Mr Knightley tries to decypher the riddle of its provenance, sensing that the piano is not from the parental Campbells but refusing to follow Emma into suspecting intrigue.

Letters, too, need interpretation. They are read and reread, are sometimes private, sometimes public, but never quite yield all their meaning, even when declared to the whole village. All of genteel Highbury hears of Jane Fairfax when she writes to Miss Bates, but no one catches her reason for not travelling to Ireland. The letters here become metonyms for their writers. Jane and Frank exist in them before ever they arrive, and they continue to live under the watchful, unobservant eyes of the community through their clandestine correspondence. Jane tries to avoid the patronising Mrs Elton by getting her own letters from the post office, so guarding her secret. Here, and elsewhere, letters have a clear material existence: at Miss Bates's, Emma is pleased to avoid the artefact even if she must hear the contents; Frank precipitates the crisis in Jane's feelings by failing to post the letter in which he counters her breaking of their engagement.

The habit of guessing and puzzling in the texture of *Emma* may influence the reader's response and lead to detection of hidden strategies. Other Austen novels such as *Pride and Prejudice* can be playfully defined in terms of secret manoeuvrings – does Charlotte scheme to attach Darcy to Elizabeth so as to advance herself and her new husband? – but the books do not demand such interpretation or their included letters such inspection. With its lack of surface story and its constant sense of undercover activities, *Emma* seems a more fruitful site.

For example, the final marriage of Harriet and Robert Martin may have been brought about by the joint act of the future Mr and Mrs George Knightley: if so, the scheming Emma would have acted inadvertently, while the Knightley brothers, those embodiments of English transparency, would have proceeded in full consciousness of their intrigue. Mr Knightley knew that Emma had prevented Harriet's acceptance of Martin's first proposal and may have intended to repair the damage. Otherwise, there is no accounting for the long conversation in which he examines Harriet's principles and even discusses agriculture with her. Presumably the purpose is to discover whether it is worth promoting her match to his tenant. It is Emma who procures the invitation from the John Knightleys to Harriet on the pretext of her needing a dentist. While she is in London, George Knightley sends Robert Martin to his brother, who purposely leaves Harriet alone with her former lover during an outing. Considering John's assertion that he never has dinner guests, the invitation to Robert Martin when Harriet is staying with his family suggests more than attractive social inclusion of someone Emma regards as much below their status. Emma and the narrator never draw attention to this manoeuvring but it seems plausible. If Mr Knightley does intrigue, it is to serve his community and also perhaps to remove another impediment to his union with Emma.

True English style

Tony Tanner has argued that *Emma* is Jane Austen's most pastoral and conservative work.[15] Certainly so if the heroine's consciousness embraces the book, for it is she who invests the unimaginative hero with her conservative vision.

Emma's appreciation of Donwell Abbey becomes part of her desire for stasis – rather like Fanny Price admiring Sotherton.

She is helped by the house itself. Unmodernised Donwell contrasts with Austen's other abbey. Northanger has modern facilities and a paraphernalia of hot and glass houses the size of a village, which allow cultivation of exotic fruit like pineapples; Donwell Abbey lacks the large public rooms that had by this period become fashionable, and its grounds provide naturalised fruit, apples, and strawberries, grown without glass houses. Where General Tilney wanted pleasing views at the expense of social feeling, Mr Knightley will not move a path to improve his meadow if it will inconvenience the Highbury villagers. He is unworried by his house's 'old neglect of prospect' and in no rush to 'improve' the pleasure grounds; his avenue of limes leads to a wall and pillars framing neither house nor view. In this carelessness, he appears a devotee less of the improver Repton, admired by Henry Crawford, than of Richard Payne Knight, who found such neglect picturesque, an expression of English freedom.

Emma invests Mr Knightley with Burkean conservative values – he heads a family of 'true gentility, untainted in blood and understanding'; but she avoids one aspect of his depiction: as a modern agriculturist, the only Austen landowner seen actually producing foodstuffs. Given eighteenth- and early nineteenth-century agricultural changes, from rotations of crops to enclosure of land, a landowning man wishing to increase or keep intact his wealth had to interest himself in the new science: indeed, the agriculturist Arthur Young noted that gentlemen who had in earlier times left matters to their stewards now managed their farms themselves and studied 'husbandry' and 'rural oeconomics'.[16] In his care and rural investment, Mr Knightley is depicted as this kind of modern gentleman. He rarely uses his horses for his carriage; presumably, with his tenant, he reads the agricultural reports, and he constantly converses on practical agricultural matters. In his lamentation for the torpidity of the rentier class, Trotter gives as his ideal the working farmer and his agrarian life. Unlike Sir Thomas of *Mansfield Park*, who lives in a modern (eighteenth-century Palladian) house and derives part of his income from exploitative colonial enterprise, Mr Knightley in economic terms is Trotter's farmer and, for all the feudal tone with which Emma tries to invest him, he even comes close to the approved worker in the radical Tom Paine's remark: 'the aristocracy are not the farmers who work the land, and raise the produce, but are the mere consumers of the rent; and when compared with the active world are the drones . . .'[17]

Mr Knightley was reputedly Austen's favourite portrait of a traditional country gentleman. If so, he seems to imply her moderate political views. He is a hereditary landowner, but neither inevitably corrupted by privilege like the radical Godwin's hereditary squire Falkland in *Caleb Williams* nor embodying a Burkean 'sure principle of conservation'.[18] Rather, he sees need for some reform – much as liberals in the post-Revolution period of war thought of England. At the same time, it is well that in the end he will marry Emma, who can leaven his agriculture with her culture, make his grounds prettier with her money, inhabit more fully his large house, afford to send more than apples to the community, and even perhaps bring in a little un-English frivolity.

For, although some critics find Jane Austen's 'authority . . . vested in Mr Knightley', he does seem somewhat limited.[19] There is no mention of a library at Donwell, although there are 'books of engravings, drawers of medals, cameos, corals, shells, and every other family collection within his cabinets', and it seems doubtful that, unlike his tenant Martin, he will aim to read the novels that engross his lady. He does not always live appropriately for his station: he often refuses to dance, something that damns Mr Darcy in a gathering with supernumerary ladies. His presenting of apples to the Bateses is kindly, but that he has none left for himself suggests he feels the need for squirely giving even when his substance cannot quite allow it. He stands on his rank when he snubs Mrs Elton with the argument that 'gentlemen and ladies, with their servants' had better eat indoors, rather than outside in fashionable mock-peasant style. He can be socially awkward; he is unnecessarily brusque about Emma's portrait of Harriet and he does not always converse when civility requires it. At times he is quite rude – almost as rude as Emma on Box Hill, if not so witty, when he snaps at Miss Bates about Jane's excessive singing: 'Are you mad?' and later talks loudly over her. At such moments he echoes his bad-mannered brother John, who can only be contained at Hartfield by Emma's soothing tact. The 'English' manner of greeting between the Knightley brothers, which Emma appreciates, draws on the French caricature of English taciturnity and bluntness, as well as on English pride in sincerity: 'John Knightley made his appearance, and "How d'ye do, George?" and "John, how are you?" succeeded in the true English style, burying under a calmness that seemed all but indifference, the real attachment which would have led either of them, if requisite, to do every thing for the good of the other' (*E*, 1:12).

Here the patriotic opinion of 'true English style' is not clearly ascribed to either the narrator or Emma, but it fits with the latter's vision of restrained parochial Englishness in Mr Knightley's grounds:

> It was a sweet view – sweet to the eye and the mind. English verdure, English culture, English comfort, seen under a sun bright, without being oppressive.   (*E*, 3:6)

The pastoral patriotism is unlike the stern moral sort implied in *Mansfield Park*, and the difference reflects a different time of writing. *Mansfield Park* was composed before the tide of war had turned in England's favour with Wellington's success in the Peninsular War. *Emma* was written in 1814–15 when prospects were hopeful and before the war's end brought the depression and disillusion that would inform *Persuasion*. Emma's vision – if it is hers alone – is of prosperity without capitalist activity; it is aestheticised in a way Mr Knightley never sees his land. Indeed, the vision is not a million miles away from the *faux rustique* countryside to be viewed from Mrs Elton's pastoral donkey. By contrast, Mr Knightley's patriotism is connected with the duty of farmers urged in the war years to maximise the yield of their land while imports were scarce.

The two visions are ironically aligned. For Emma is actually looking not at Donwell Abbey and its immediate grounds but at its tenancy, Abbey-Mill Farm, home of the Martins, the place it would have degraded Harriet to inhabit. This farm is not just a pastoral example, 'safely viewed with all its appendages of prosperity and beauty, its rich pastures, spreading flocks, orchard in blossom, and light column of smoke ascending', but also a sign of the rise of what Emma has called a 'yeoman' to the status of Mr Knightley's 'gentleman farmer' during this final period of the war, when internal prices were high.[20] The prosperous farm embodies the kind of aspiration that most agitates Emma's social vision, the encroaching of lower classes, the changing of place.

And anxiety sometimes seeps into Emma's perception even of Donwell Abbey, when, like Elizabeth Bennet observing Pemberley, she imagines a mistress for the house and grounds: 'Jane Fairfax mistress of the Abbey! Oh! no, no; – every feeling revolts . . . A Mrs. Knightley for them all to give way to!' Yet Jane is elegant and accomplished and would as little degrade Donwell Abbey as Abbey-Mill Farm would degrade Harriet. Again it seems that pastoral perfection needs impossible stasis and framing by a self-satisfied onlooker. The complacency about English 'comfort' is also much modified by Jane herself, who, her heart wrung by Frank, actually flees from Donwell Abbey in misery.

Emma is not entirely contained in her 'English' vision either. For all her holding to Highbury ways, she feels the alien fascination of Frank Churchill as Mr Knightley never does. To her he is not just the prized son of the village but – and here his first name comes into play – a contrast to the very English *George* Knightley in his stagey French flirtatiousness, his fashionable triviality and ennui, his deceit, restlessness, and rootlessness. He is even 'sick of England', a statement made just after Emma sees the apotheosis of Englishness at Donwell.[21] '[N]ot quite the thing' is perhaps Mr Woodhouse's most perceptive judgement in the novel. Yet Emma sees her kinship with this foreign-inflected young man. She suspects that he has enjoyed deceiving Highbury over his engagement to Jane Fairfax and admits she, too, might have done so in his place.

But he took her hand

After being unloved by two supposed lovers, Mr Elton and Frank Churchill, Emma receives as lover a man who allows her to be a daughter at Hartfield and the wife of a virile working man. He is strangely introduced. Unlike Willoughby, Darcy, or Wentworth, Mr Knightley enters quietly: 'a visitor . . . walked in'. Initial remarks are cool. Having had no 'charm' thrown over his senses – in the manner he observes in Mrs Weston and which trapped Edmund for Mary Crawford – he would rather like to see Emma in love but unsure of a return. He appears more brother and father than lover, and Mrs Weston, eager to find a mate for her favourite, never lights on the neighbourhood's most eligible bachelor. When Emma boasts of her match-making over the previous four years, Mr Knightley exclaims, 'a worthy employment for a young lady's mind!' She responds, 'And you have never known the pleasure and triumph of a lucky guess? – I pity you. – I thought you cleverer' (*E*, 1:1). The exchange has something of the impudent flirtation of Elizabeth and Darcy but is more barbed, more embedded in familial habit. *Mansfield Park* opens with the insistence that the ultimate, quasi-incestuous love of cousins raised together is unlikely to take place; in *Emma* no such discussion occurs, but, as in *Sense and Sensibility*, the male lover's greater age is stressed, as is Mr Knightley's status as Emma's elder 'brother', who knew her from an infant. So the final marriage seems as familial as romantic, and so much follows the *éclaircissement* that it loses any novelty.

Emma and Mr Knightley repeatedly misconstrue each other: when Emma had watched him conversing with Harriet, she had erroneously thought he was, first, being kind and, second, falling in love, when he was in fact discovering her good principles. These he praises Emma for helping instil; she accepts the compliment, knowing she has done no such thing. Indeed, she has actually inflated Harriet out of her becoming modesty into a belief in her worthiness for the highest match in the community. Emma and Mr Knightley intend to treat each other with 'full and perfect confidence', doing away with all mystery, but they begin marriage with the husband's ignorance of his wife's bizarre suspicions about himself, Harriet, and Jane. Mr Knightley's sturdy belief in transparency remains the best ideal on offer perhaps, but needs qualifying. Emma had been close to truth with Miss Bates on Box Hill: that was the problem. As the narrator remarks: 'Seldom, very seldom, does complete truth belong to any human disclosure' (*E*, 3:13).

The union of Emma and Mr Knightley may, then, appear only marginally better in Emma's mind (and the reader's) than the amicable singleness of both. The counterfactual of Emma's life has none of the horror Fanny Price felt when she contemplated what existence might have been with Henry Crawford. Emma would have had a different life without Knightley, but she was already preparing for it in her usual exaggerated way when he proposed. Her days would have been 'inferior in spirit and gaiety' but she would have become more 'rational', more self-aware, combining some repression with some self-knowledge; and she would have spent time reading those ignored lists, or have meant to. It is not so different from her proposed future *with* Mr Knightley: 'What had she to wish for? Nothing, but to grow more worthy of him, whose intentions and judgment had been ever so superior to her own. Nothing, but that the lessons of her past folly might teach her humility and circumspection in future' (*E*, 3:18). As in *Mansfield Park*, the narrator hides the declaration scene, but the reticence is more intrusive here: 'what did she say? just what she ought of course, a lady always does'. It is bathos from a supremely stylish author, irritating to most readers and going beyond her usual recoil from directly delivered feeling. The 'perfect happiness of the union' at the end cannot avoid recalling Austen's impatience with any 'pictures of perfection' and Mr Knightley's annoyance on Box Hill when in response to Mr Weston's riddle – 'What two letters of the alphabet are there, that express perfection?' (the answer being M A) – he remarks, '*Perfection* should not have come quite so soon' (*E*, 3:7).

The marriage is a satisfying *community* affair in which Emma consolidates her status.[22] As the only heroine in the position to contribute financially to the improvement of an estate, she will donate her £30,000 to ease the problems of Donwell – Mr Knightley has 'little spare money'. The social status quo will be sensitively maintained now Emma's fearful expectations of adult life have been exploded – and she has managed to marry while staying 'married' to her father. Presumably snobbery will be collective if restrained (neither thinks a girl like Harriet, without birth, good enough for a gentleman clergyman, and both tend to equate Miss Bates's status with her income). Mr Knightley's patriarchal notions of marriage have been dented by his choice of a wife without a 'delightful inferiority', one who will not, like Mrs Weston and Isabella, constantly respond to the moods of her husband, and he will make the sacrifice of moving from his masculine domain into Hartfield, despite his opinion that 'A man would always wish to give a woman a better home than the one he takes her from' (*E*, 3:13). Emma will not experience what Mrs. Elton calls 'one of the evils of matrimony'; instead she will fulfil her father's opening opinion *à propos* of Mrs Weston, that a married woman does not need 'a house of her own', especially if she is 'first' in the familial one. Emma will bring her female skill to bear on their joint life. Although occasionally tactless outside, she is a constant social facilitator at Hartfield, both gracious and diplomatic; she can now use this skill to patronise two villages. Her fantasy life may continue, but she has found that she must make do emotionally with what is in front of her, as she rationally made do with the view from Ford's: Mr Knightley was in front of her eyes from the start. It all seems very cool, and the concluding wedding, mocked by Mrs Elton for its lack of finery, is almost a parody of romantic glamour.

Yet love seeps in. Not the hungry repressed sort of Fanny Price or Mr Darcy but something more mutual and unexpected. It is adumbrated in the way each keeps tabs on the other. When Emma and Harriet discuss a conversation about spruce beer, Emma remembers exactly where Mr Knightley was standing, while he looks sourly at Frank Churchill for little other reason than that he seems licensed to flirt with Emma. Needing no arrow of sudden perception to realise his affection, he claims to have loved her since she was thirteen and, echoing many eighteenth-century romances (of the sort he clearly does not read), to have loved her because of her faults.[23] His saving of a reading list for some time resembles Harriet's keeping of Mr Elton's 'court plaister' and pencil stub, while something of Fanny Price emerges in his anxiety that a familial mentoring relationship may not easily be made amorous.

On her side, like her predecessors, Emma is given the physical language of feeling and, despite her cerebral life, she looks to her body for guidance when thinking of love. Presumably from the romantic fiction she has read with Harriet, she has grasped the signs and she scrutinises herself for them: can she see 'listlessness, weariness, stupidity,' she asks when she thinks of Frank Churchill. The answer is No. Instead, the first time her body opens to emotion is when Mr Knightley rebukes her for rudeness to Miss Bates at Box Hill and the tears run unchecked down her cheek. When a repentant Emma is discovered compensating for her lapse, Mr Knightley replies with a 'glow'. An erotic charge surges from the pain, and the pair move so close that physical boundaries disappear; the moment is captured in the fractured syntax Austen will later fully develop to express deep emotion in *Persuasion*: 'He took her hand; – whether she had not herself made the first motion, she could not say – she might, perhaps, have rather offered it – but he took her hand' (*E*, 3:9). (It is not clear why he drops it – perhaps he fears he will kiss it and appear Frenchified.)

In some ways, Emma's love has a rather 'unnatural beginning' – to use Anne Elliot's later phrase for the trajectory of her emotions in *Persuasion* – for it appears that she began taking her prudential ownership of Mr Knightley for granted even before she fell in love with him. When, knowing more of her own heart, she fears that he is pursuing Harriet, Emma is presented as unable to be still: she starts, sighs, and walks about, stands and sits – echoing unawares the moving misery of Jane Fairfax when her engagement was broken. Body and mind unite to feel the arrow of desire and, when she knows it reciprocal, her body flashes out: she who had been so often stopped by her coercing father from dancing is now 'in dancing, singing, exclaiming spirits'. The love of Mr Knightley becomes her 'fever' and the assurance of it makes for a 'sleepless night'. Motherhood, once rejected, forms part of her new erotic vision: remembering her earlier concern for the rights of her nephew as heir of Donwell, she gives herself 'a saucy conscious smile', and her desire for a daughter for Mrs Weston argues a son for herself (even her new-found erotic feelings fail to break her habit of plotting and imagining other people's romantic possibilities). The triangle of desire, so potent in *Mansfield Park*, serves here as well: Emma loves Mr Knightley in part because she unconsciously feared Jane Fairfax was her rival, and because she consciously wants to make her second supposed rival – her once 'intimate friend' Harriet – into 'nothing'. While she asserts she *must* have Mr Knightley, she desires him still to be mastering; echoing Mary Crawford's wish to control the 'sturdy' Edmund, when married Emma wants her husband to remain 'Mr Knightley'.

Chapter 8

Persuasion

The accident of death makes *Persuasion* Jane Austen's final novel. It deserves its position by its innovative treatment of passion and rhetorical style as well as its development of those themes of memory and time, public and private history, inner and outer lives, language and literature, emotion and restraint that have marked all Austen's previous works. In its wistful longing to privatise a public state, it relates most to the concerns of *Mansfield Park*, while its depiction of emotional tumult recalls *Sense and Sensibility*.

Persuasion opens with 'tangled, useless histories of the family in the first fifty pages', as an exasperated Maria Edgeworth commented.[1] This past meticulously roots the heroine within her noble family's genealogy, only progressively to reveal it as meaningless to her. Like the preceding novels, *Persuasion* considers home and homecoming, but, where they move towards a new or renewed symbolic and physical home for the heroine, this last completed work begins with her ejection and ends with her understanding that home is not a place at all but an ambience and an acceptance of change. Considering the Burkean association of the nation with the hereditary estate, the perception qualifies the patriotism of British victory which also emerges from the novel.

Jane Austen began work on *Persuasion* in August 1815, just as Napoleon sailed to exile in St Helena following his defeat at Waterloo. She ended the first draft in August 1816, when the initial excitement had subsided and the results of twenty-two years of war were being assessed: the economic cost – Britain had an immense national debt with high taxes to service it – and the political price of government-imposed national unity through years of patriotic propaganda. If *Mansfield Park* might be termed a 'state of the nation' work, *Persuasion* might be a 'Waterloo novel', although the battle occurs outside its frame: Austen's contribution to the debate about the new society coming into being through peace. If so, again like *Mansfield Park*, the work expresses its vision obliquely, using the domestic relationships that must underpin, but may not easily influence, any civil and social order.

On 13 March 1817 Austen wrote, 'I have a something ready for Publication, which may perhaps appear about a twelvemonth hence' (*L*, p. 333), a statement which suggests she was intending either revision or a lengthy process of publication. The former suggestion has led critics to speculate about what she would have changed. They focus on the occasional unsentimental harshness and abrupt transitions which make the novel seem a decline from *Mansfield Park* and *Emma*, the slow beginning beside the abrupt synopsis of the ending, the undeveloped characters like Mr Shepherd, and undeveloped relationships like Sir Walter Elliot's with Mrs Clay. Certainly *Persuasion* is less technically brilliant than its immediate predecessors and more polarised in its presentation of satire and sentiment; yet many readers prefer it to all other Austen novels and find its haunting quality little disturbed by awkwardness in plot or incident.

The unfeudal tone

The book might have been called 'The Elliots' – Cassandra claimed this was the most discussed option – implying a group portrait like *Mansfield Park*, although in the end substituting a family of inclination for a claustrophobic blood one. But Henry Austen, who saw it through publication after Jane's death, probably chose the more suggestive *Persuasion*, which draws attention to the novel's pervasive theme of literary and social influence and suited the current fashion for abstract titles like Edgeworth's *Patronage* and Brunton's *Discipline*.

The work contrasts with its predecessor in hero and heroine. The snobbish, conservative, landlocked Emma, who stays at home even after marriage, opposes Anne Elliot, homeless and alienated from her family (the two novels momentarily come together when Emma faces a spinster's life in her father's house), while Captain Wentworth is far from the traditional Mr Knightley – here the hereditary landlord is Mr Elliot, the hollow heir of Kellynch. A candid man of action, an adventurer interested in career and money, Captain Wentworth is the sort of figure who, like Wickham and Frank Churchill in previous novels, has crashed in from elsewhere to unsettle the heroine, a glamorous, ballad warrior who returns to find a sweetheart. In social terms, *Persuasion* contrasts with all other Austen novels, being the first in which the heroine, choosing such a man, marries downward and out of the gentry class, facing, even with his 'independent fortune', a financially unstable life. Outside the protagonists there is no village community, no one who much cares whether a particular squire is present or absent; Highbury and Mansfield are replaced by the shifting society of the navy, whose home is the sea and seaside lodgings and whose cementing talk is of shared encounters and exotic places. In contrast, land society displays only empty rituals of meeting and mourning.

Persuasion is a nostalgic text, stirred by both the warring past and a future of uncharted change, and it refers directly to events in the way no other of Jane Austen's books has done. Here, the patriotism of individual moral effort and of comfortable 'English verdure' no longer suffices for a victorious nation which needs to address its social fissures and accept a new 'unfeudal tone'. Samuel Bamford, a radical weaver, remarked that 'whilst the laurels were yet cool on the brows of our victorious soldiers . . . the elements of convulsion were at work among the masses of our labouring population'.[2] Although there is no dwelling on the miseries of the poor or the polarising of new politicised classes, *Persuasion* implies a need for some change in attitude. The Burkean line of great houses stretching from *Sense and Sensibility*'s Norland through Pemberley to Mansfield Park and Donwell Abbey ends in Kellynch Hall, up for rent with the contemptuous remark: 'they were gone who deserved not to stay, and . . . Kellynch-Hall had passed into better hands than its owners'.

The tenant, Admiral Croft, representing new money and an entrepreneurial naval spirit, removes the looking-glasses that once reflected the static self of Sir Walter Elliot and shifts the umbrellas to beside the entrance, so servants do not always have to fetch them and make a parade of hierarchy. But he is paying money for the privilege of living like a gentleman and is willing to move out if the traditional gentry can afford to return; Kellynch will revert to its owners and the future, including the morally bankrupt though well-bred Mr Elliot, promises none of the renewal suggested for Donwell Abbey and Pemberley.

The novel exists in two times, 1806, the much remembered year in which Anne Elliot and Frederick Wentworth met and fell in love, and 1814–15 during the temporary peace when he returns. This stretched between Napoleon's defeat and exile to Elba in April 1814 and his escape and return to Paris followed by renewed war early in 1815. Then for a few weeks military men would be wanted again, although only the author and readers know this. Wentworth and Anne are thus embedded in history, their own and the nation's. Other Elliots hardly seem to notice the momentous times since, unlike Anne and her friend Lady Russell (and indeed the narrow Mr Price of *Mansfield Park*), they read no pamphlets and newspapers and have forgotten the navy's contribution to the life they are still privileged to lead. Sir Walter peruses only the backward-looking *Baronetage*, which traces families from the creation of the rank in the early seventeenth century; he and his eldest daughter (his surrogate wife, rather like Emma with Mr Woodhouse) cannot understand an unsettled country or see their own failure in historic rather than genealogical terms.

Like Elizabeth Bennet and Emma, the heroine Anne Elliot feels the seduction of the great house; when Mr Elliot pays his court, the vision of being mistress of

Kellynch momentarily 'bewitches' her and intrudes the memory of her mother as worthy lady of the manor – it is a 'charm which she could not immediately resist'. The notion of the landed gentry with its responsibilities is still important to Anne, who is appalled at how little her father thinks of them when he worries only about his pleasure grounds and grows proud of his ostentatious lodgings in Bath. But she withstands the 'charm' for a more economically imprudent love, which earlier heroines had found less potent. Thinking of Mr Elliot, she considers the human legacy of marrying an unprincipled man – as her mother had done, leaving on her death three daughters to be damaged by an inadequate spouse. At the end of the novel there is, uniquely in Austen, no indication of where the hero and heroine will live, no promise of mansion or improved parsonage.

Thoroughly aware of the impinging of national on local concerns, Anne is attuned to cultural change. She sees Kellynch turn from a gentleman's seat into rental property, and notices the furniture of Uppercross Cottage and the Great House becoming shabby and outmoded while the daughters clutter formal eighteenth-century spaces with nineteenth-century *bric-à-brac*. Home becomes, in her mind, a place inhabited by affectionate people, anywhere unchilled by the Elliot presence. The snug ships find their counterpart in the rooms made watertight by a sailor's handiwork, as if the Harvilles' Lyme lodgings were a kind of beached vessel. As in *Pride and Prejudice*, the heroine looks at the space the hero inhabits, finds what she lacks and knows she desires; her desire no longer includes the great house of Kellynch.

Nina Auerbach argues that *Persuasion* presents a vision of the navy as a 'brave new world', its triumph a 'revolution of values' in favour of the 'utopian hopes' of Romanticism.[3] It is hard for us to see as revolutionary a service whose policing includes the re-establishment of the corrupt political order of Europe and the quashing of dissent at home, or to find idealism in men who seem more interested in personal gain than national victory. Yet the book does give some of the moral significance partly vested in the clergy in *Mansfield Park* and the 'untainted' landowner in *Emma* to this meritocratic profession, or rather not to the navy itself, but to individual naval men – the admiralty is as corrupt as any other ruling order. The ending claims 'domestic virtues' for naval officers, and depiction of their shipboard life and camaraderie supports this. Sir Walter Elliot and his son-in-law Charles Musgrove cannot easily appreciate men without property, men whose property is in themselves; proud that he has earned 'every blessing' he enjoys, Wentworth has 'nothing but himself to recommend him'. The novel suggests that, although he may be temporarily humbled in regards to Anne, this particular 'nothing' is 'something': it is the Elliots' grand relatives, the Dalrymples, who are dismissed as 'nothing'. Mary Crawford's denigration of the professions is here echoed only in the shallow Mrs Clay's remark, that professional men lose their 'personableness'.

However, on land, where subtlety and compromise are needed, these martial sailors are often inept. Wentworth is poor at judging people – Louisa, for example, and Captain Benwick. As Anne remarks when her lover assumes her actions at nineteen and twenty-seven would be identical, 'You should have distinguished.' Both Wentworth and Benwick, veterans of sea battles, are portrayed as helpless before one unconscious girl. It seems that much of the heroic glow surrounding the officers comes not from anything we see them do but from Anne's admiring and loving consciousness – rather as Emma invests Mr Knightley with her nostalgic vision of England – for the navy has formed her mental life for the past eight years. As she once implicitly defended a Burkean vision of a hereditary estate by carefully cataloguing the ancestral contents of Kellynch and fulfilling its community duties, so now she supports a vision of the navy as guardian of the nation and the peace. Almost her first words praise the service, and the novel's last words encapsulate her view of combined domestic virtues and 'national importance'.

Through her heroine's manifest admiration Jane Austen here seems trying to reverse a national trend.[4] In 1805, when Nelson won the battle of Trafalgar and saved England from French invasion, the navy achieved great prestige but, although it continued to be the main source of British war power over the next years, its cultural status diminished when it failed to win further substantial victories, not even in the American War of 1812. In contrast, the victorious army under the Duke of Wellington had won the Peninsular War and would go on to the success of Waterloo. The national response emerges in *Sanditon* where the entrepreneurial Mr Parker wishes he had not named his boarding-house Trafalgar but waited for Wellington's later victory. Writing *Don Juan* in September 1818, Lord Byron noted the waning popularity of the navy and the ease with which the public forgot past achievements: 'There's no more to be said of Trafalgar / 'Tis with our hero quietly inurn'd' (I, iv). On 8 May 1815 appeared a caricature, *Things as they have been. Things as they now are*, showing a naval officer in two parts: one smart and assertive, the other more downtrodden.[5] Admiral Croft and his brother-in-law escaped this fate: they were lucky, making money and suffering none of the debilitating shipboard diseases Sir Walter expects, while Admiral Croft is also associated with the glamour of Trafalgar. Now in 1814, with his prize money – in the book no moral opprobrium attends this piratical activity of catching martial and commercial boats – Wentworth is himself a 'prize' in the marriage market, while the high-ranking Elliots have fallen on hard times.[6] He has even acquired some of the patina of a gentleman and has none of the nautical quirks of Admiral Croft. However, he lacks the 'politeness and suavity' of Mr Elliot, that 'gentleman in manner' (qualities which Darcy had to learn in *Pride and Prejudice)*. At the end he has the wife of his heart but no inherited property to look forward to – as his future sister-in-law Mary smugly notes. He remains a naval officer on half-pay, expecting future commissions.

Despite Captain Harville's limp and the mention of one or two dead friends, the war appears the source less of injury and death than of opportunity for clever or brave young men to rise through merit. Indeed, it seems more perilous to be a civilian in the world of *Persuasion*.[7] Lady Elliot, Mr Elliot's rich wife, and Benwick's beloved Fanny Harville all die, while a crucial event is the injury of Louisa Musgrove, who, trying to impress Captain Wentworth by the 'firmness' she believes he wants, jumps once too often from the Cobb in Lyme Regis. She seems first 'dead' (Mary Musgrove's melodramatic word), then damaged: she recovers but will remain nervous and 'altered', fit lover for the emotional Benwick, who will, through his miniature, get himself new 'set' for his new love. (For Wentworth the blow he indirectly provokes has the contrary effect on his own head, for it brings him back to his original rational senses.) At home, the Musgrove heir has a dangerous accident and breaks his collar bone. Beyond these extreme events there is physical vulnerability quite different from that of war.[8] It starts with Sir Walter looking with distaste on his thin, faded daughter Anne, continues through the unwanted freckles in the widow Mrs Clay, to the crippling rheumatism of Anne's old school-friend Mrs Smith. The miseries of war are subsumed into the general human proneness to damage and death. The environment qualifies Admiral Croft's unseemly remark about 'the good luck' of another war.

The navy is attractive through its defined hierarchy, relative mobility, and partial ignoring of birth. It becomes ironic then that, at the end, the sailor Wentworth helps Mrs Smith re-enter the propertied class from which his own wife will fall. Land society is far from fluid. Even in her lowly position, Mrs Smith held to her original middle-class status by bountifully giving away what little she earned, and she declared she could not have known Mr Elliot's wife since she was so ill-born and -bred. Despite her up-to-date reading and awareness of the outside world, Lady Russell, as a knight's lady, is too impressed with the hereditary rank of the absurd Sir Walter, too unappreciative of any 'tone' outside the feudal one, and her sensible advice about Wentworth in 1806 had been marked by this outlook. She despises Mrs Clay for her status as well as her character as the kind of improperly flattering friend Mr Knightley disapproves in *Emma*. Anne's dislike is in part fear of a social manipulator cannier than herself, but it, too, is class-based and appears before Mrs Clay has displayed poor morals – indeed, Anne's dismissive attitude prevents her from seeing signs of intrigue between Mrs Clay and Mr Elliot.

The holding to rank can become indecorous. Mary, the least attractive daughter of the 'spendthrift baronet', insists on precedence over her kindly mother-in-law and fears that Wentworth might be elevated to the baronetcy, so rendering less exclusive the rank that provides her status.[9] In Bath, her father and sister, through employing unnecessary servants and stage-managing their lives and lodgings, try in their few rooms to recreate the appearance of importance lost when they gave up the hereditary estate. It is fitting that their stay occurs when Bath is past its prime, more retreat than modish resort: in his obsession with rank and manners, Sir Walter is an anachronism, weirdly unageing – in his own eyes anyway – in the nineteenth century.

In *Emma*, rank had hidden the disadvantages of gender from the heroine. In *Persuasion*, a constant debate about gendered roles is staged, through the depiction both of traditional families and hereditary houses and of the new shifting world of 1815 and returning self-made men. Anne shows what happens when the gender divide is strictly followed: she watches her stupider father destroy the basis of her Kellynch home. Supporting this implied critique is Wentworth's initially shallow and confused notion of women. When he sees Anne again, he thinks only of her appearance, then turns a careless attention to the trivial but pleasing Musgrove girls as if they were another species. Either would do for him according to the admiral. Believing that Anne had been 'weak' to refuse him and yet holding her as his ideal, he wants women to add to their 'sweet' femininity the masculine quality of steadfastness, which, given his restricted idea of their activities, can only show itself in tomboyish or perverse actions.

His sister, the 'square', slightly Amazonian Mrs Croft, who has sailed with her husband – a choice her brother condemns – is Wentworth's antidote. Neatly destabilising the gendered division of intellectual and emotional labour, she excels the blinkered, good-natured admiral in traditionally masculine areas of life. She is more prudent and sensible, knows more about driving and finance (similar here to Lady Russell in relation to Sir Walter), and she is as 'intelligent and keen as any of the officers'. (On the other side, Captain Harville fashions toys and netting needles. Discussing naval education, Maria Edgeworth's father, Richard Lovell Edgeworth, urged training with carpenter's, smith's, and turner's tools to keep the sailor occupied onshore;[10] so this is not 'women's work' but it has a domestic air.)

A feminist case may be implied by Mrs Croft and the depiction of the professional Nurse Rooke, who, although in a lowly position, combines the practical and psychological abilities that argue women's fitness to be physicians. But, although they impinge on the portrait of the heroine, they do not govern it. Anne does indeed gain some of the admirable Mrs Croft's freedom and it remains significant that the only sign in the novel of her new status as chosen woman is not a house but a means of transport, a smart landaulette.[11] And yet the childless Mrs Croft baulks at the traditionally female role of watcher and waiter, falling ill when left alone and unoccupied, where Anne has survived many years of such existence. The heroine may live onboard as Austen's sister-in-law did when Charles's ship was in home waters but, as a future mother, is unlikely to go to sea, and the final paragraph suggests an onshore wife paying the 'tax' of anxiety about a wandering spouse.[12] When Wentworth moves towards Anne, he has to forego some of his traditional assumptions, but not women's role as familial nurses – indeed he shows his first real gentleness and 'glow' towards her when he sees her supporting the stricken Louisa. Anne's instinctive nursing skills and service role of comforter and facilitator relate her less to the professional nurse, whom she fails even to notice, and more to Mrs Harville (herself of lower social standing). If she joins a 'profession', like Fanny Price it is as suitable wife.

A little history

Pride and Prejudice and *Mansfield Park* were concerned with the subjectivity of time and the malleability of memory. *Persuasion* develops this investigation. Anne Elliot's mind is preoccupied with what the narrator calls her 'little history of sorrowful interest'. Although it remains the characters' secret, only fitfully disclosed, and the story-telling hero represses before he recoups it, this romantic 'history' determines Anne's life in the present, and the eight years since it occurred have almost no story. All the reader knows is that the love of 1806 began as a social commonplace, for 'he had nothing to do and she had hardly any body to love'.

In the intervening years most people have aged. Sailors return unrecognisable to the preserved Sir Walter, while Lady Russell moves from prospective partner to old woman who should wear more make-up.[13] Like Anne, Lady Russell has an acute sense of time passing, noting the difference between her friend at nineteen, the optimum time to attract a husband it seems, and twenty-two when she feels that boorish, good-natured Charles Musgrove might do, and twenty-seven when she joins Anne in near hopelessness. There is more stress on precise age here than in any previous novel, more noting of numbers and dates, of specific years and repeated seasons, suggesting always the melancholy passage of time which war and peace, marriage and death never interrupt.

The present of the book begins with Sir Walter contemplating the fixed image of himself in the *Baronetage*, past words controlling his present. His daughter Anne mirrors him for she is equally static, as fixated on the *Navy Lists* as her father on the 'Book of Books', and she emerges only in spurts from this stasis. The novel discovers her alone in autumn, feeling herself one with the declining year, her 'bloom' gone with the single, romantic summer. While she is given more acute sensory impressions than any earlier heroine, her head is filled with the past or a distant naval present rather than with day-to-day events nearby. She has let her life be blighted by a single time, a blight which would have continued but for the accident of Admiral Croft renting her father's house and inviting Captain Wentworth to visit. In a letter to her niece Fanny Knight in 1814 advising her to give up a young man if she does not care for him, whatever *he* may be supposed to feel, Jane Austen denies that people die of a broken heart: 'it is no creed of mine . . . that such sort of Disappointments kill anybody' (*L*, p. 281). In *Persuasion*, Anne is not far from being killed by romance in a way refused to Marianne Dashwood as she submitted at nineteen 'to new attachments' and followed the 'natural sequence' from romance to prudence. From the same age Anne grows more estranged and the first part of the novel presents as vivid a picture of depression as early fiction contains.[14] It is in keeping with a contemporary psychological view that 'Representations of the mind, when frequently renewed by acts of the imagination, at last acquire a degree of vividness which surpasses those derived from external objects.'[15]

The 'romance', a word here used (newly for Austen) with little ironic overtone, has been 'renewed' in memory and become Anne's burden. She has chosen to be a person who waits and looks, reads and lives in books and silent words, and does not dance, so removing herself from the world of courtship the dance floor signifies. (Fittingly, at the rapturous end her 'spirits' go 'dancing' as young Emma's do when she knows herself loved.) She moves quietly round the houses of relatives and friends and for a large part of the first volume speaks hardly a word. Despite being embedded in a numerous family, whether alone or in crowded rooms she exudes solitude; as a result, even Lady Russell is unaware of the extent of her devotion to the past.

Anne Elliot is the most self-conscious of Austen's heroines, existing within a book which stays close to her consciousness – it enters Captain Wentworth's only once to capture his continued bitterness and assumption that his love is dead. She labours to repress feelings while valuing spontaneous bursts of emotion in others. Even more than Fanny Price with her suspicion of her own motives, Anne is represented as correcting her attitudes with intense and occasionally ironic awareness. Often she has to retreat to prepare her mind in private for the self-control her chosen path demands, then brace herself for the little public scrutiny she will attract. As a result of such rigorous fading, she has diminished any influence she might have with her father and sister. Outside the immediate family she continues withdrawn: seeing the damage Wentworth is unthinkingly inflicting on Charles Hayter, Henrietta Musgrove's suitor, she 'longed for the power of representing to them all what they were about', but she keeps quiet.

Thinking always of her short time of happiness, she is yet presented as fearing the 'oblivion of the past' – after all, she sees her family 'oblivious' of her former engagement. When she meets Wentworth again, it sometimes seems that he intrudes on a sacred memory.[16] Where time may move for him – 'What might not eight years do?' – it stays still for her: 'eight years may be little more than nothing' (P, 1:7). Anne is sure that the past cannot be replicated in the future because she and Wentworth have become 'strangers' in 'perpetual estrangement'. Yet she allows his little act of kindness in placing her in the Crofts' carriage to be 'a reminder of former sentiment'.[17]

The two-volume structure of the novel, with emotional descent in the first, ascent in the second, emphasises the final move to Bath. While never obliterating Anne's passionate memory, change of place loosens its hold and pain is 'softened'. Thus she begins a process of unfreezing the present which starts to mitigate the 'perpetual estrangement'. Before arriving in Bath, Anne had feared the worst: she had been unhappy at boarding school there after her mother's death and, we might infer, in her winter with Lady Russell after Wentworth's exit had romantically reprised her maternal loss. The city represents 'glare', meaningless bustle, and snobbish jockeying for place. Yet, paradoxically, it will be the site of Anne's ultimate happiness, and its anonymous, crowded streets prepare her for the crowded, shifting lodgings of naval life – in contrast to Fanny Price's quiet future far removed from the cramped naval space of Portsmouth.

Overall change emerges from interaction not only of time and place but also of body and mind: Anne's frequent 'agitation' connects the two. In the 1790s *Sense and Sensibility*, Marianne fell ill under the emotional stress of losing Willoughby, and her sensibility was expressed in her body as well as her language and ethical code. With Trotter, however, there was a subtle shift to a more intimate interaction of mind and body, and *Persuasion* responds to this thinking. Once she leaves Kellynch and Uppercross for the resort of Lyme, out of season in cold November, Anne's body begins to react under natural and human stimuli. She is invigorated by the sea air, the kind that brings life and proper ageing in life. (Against this the attenuated Sir Walter obsessively guards, remarking, 'I have been long perfectly convinced . . . that the sea is very rarely of use to any body.')

As a result of the colour the wind has put in her cheeks, Anne becomes again visible to men: Mr Elliot glances at her admiringly and Wentworth catches the glance – and she sees that he has. Soon Lady Russell notices an improvement in 'plumpness and looks'; under the seaside influence, even querulous Mary grows less self-obsessed. The two younger Elliot sisters together exemplify Trotter's medical theory: they are dispirited women who have led too restricted lives and who gain spirits with a change of air.[18] As they should, for Trotter believes that cheerfulness is a personal patriotic duty. Depression or nervous disorder 'inevitably sap[s] our physical strength of constitution; make[s] us into a nation of slaves and ideots'.[19] Fittingly, the military men Anne admires are associated with the bracing sea. Anne regains knowledge of her own sexuality and this allows Wentworth to realise his own rekindled or – as he will claim – always existing love.

Through all Jane Austen's novels has run a theme of the mind's involvement in literature, sometimes insufficient, sometimes overwhelming. Allied to the simpler eighteenth-century anxiety over the effect of seductive novels on conduct, the use of poetry in *Persuasion* seems rather to comment on the Romantic idea of the 'creation' of life's emotion through powerful books. In the walk to Winthrop, Anne's depression is shown as exacerbated and consoled by eighteenth-century reflective nature poetry, of William Cowper, James Beattie, and Charlotte Smith, with its elegiac dissociation of natural seasons and human life: 'Another May new buds and flowers shall bring; / Ah! why has happiness – no second Spring?'[20] In Anne, assimilated quotations aestheticise and romanticise the pain of change and decay and make her accept single human seasons. The idea inevitably recurs in the verses written about Napoleonic battles, and it would have been an unusual reader in 1818 who, following Anne's musings, would not have brought to mind the elegiac martial theme of lives that could not be renewed, while the grass springs up on battlefields.

Outside elegiac pastoral, however, there are other ways of looking, and these Anne adopts in Lyme and Bath. When she saw herself as ageing and autumnal, a farmer, observing the land rather than its people, regarded autumn as a recurrent stage, and meant 'to have spring again'.[21] The early nineteenth century was fascinated by hot-house cultivation, especially of flowers which could be forced into unseasonable blooming and decay. Anne will never again be nineteen and the past years are lost, but her fading in the hot-house environment of Kellynch may be unnatural because premature: she can learn to 'bloom' again. In Lyme she advises Captain Benwick not to luxuriate in the melancholy Romantic poetry of Scott and Byron, which allows both an indulgence in grief and a heroising of pain; Byron's heroes, Conrad and the Giaour, are men who glory in their refusal to be comforted after loss. Then in Bath, talking with Captain Harville, she renounces literature altogether as the *prime* tool for interpreting real life. The pen which she has been following has been mainly in men's hands, she claims, and, as she speaks against its authority, it literally falls from Wentworth's grasp.

Dear self is concerned

'What wild imaginations one forms, where dear self is concerned!' Mrs Smith exclaims. Misreading Anne's sparkling eyes as love for Mr Elliot, she is prepared, for her own advantage, to let her old school-friend enter what Colonel Brandon in *Sense and Sensibility* called 'the worst and most irremediable of evils, a connection, for life, with an unprincipled man'. Yet Anne sees something more inspiring in her friend than self-interest. Mrs Smith is resilient because, like Elizabeth Bennet, she lives mainly in the present moment. Widowed, crippled, and poor, she is only occasionally depressed. Anne contemplates the phenomenon, aware of her own depressive years. She concludes that some of Mrs Smith's strength is due to her own efforts, to that inner struggle that Anne also wages to conform herself to her principles. But Mrs Smith has something more: 'that elasticity of mind, that disposition to be comforted, that power of turning readily from evil to good, and of finding employment which carried her out of herself, which was from Nature alone' (*P*, 2:5). Such 'elasticity' is an amoral aspect of personality rather like Emma Woodhouse's good health and vitality – and the term contrasts with the rigidity Wentworth thinks he wants in a woman. Yet, neither elasticity nor rigidity is deep feeling, and Anne's 'dear self' intrudes in her realisation that she would not trade her 'elegant and cultivated mind' for the apparent contentment of any of her friends.

Despite Jane Austen's remark that her heroine was 'almost too good' for her, Anne is no 'picture of perfection' (*L*, p. 335). She accepts ill treatment without protesting, but she notices it. She smiles in contempt at her less sensitive and subtle relatives, and has little genuine charity of heart where they are concerned, eager in an almost authorial way to 'show them what they were'. She is civil and secretive, yet condemns her cousin for his reserve. When Louisa Musgrove falls and it is unclear whether she will live or die, at this moment of most distress Anne thinks of herself and Wentworth, almost gloating that he would now know the difference between obstinacy and steadiness. From then on, her vitality increases; hearing that Louisa has become engaged to Benwick, again Anne immediately thinks of Wentworth – the colour rushes to her cheeks and she feels 'senseless joy'. Cunningly she seeks information to please herself, asking the Crofts what Wentworth said about the engagement, trying to gauge his feelings for her through his disparaging remarks about another. (In much the same way she denies Mr Elliot's interest in her when he has virtually proposed, so that she learns the truth of his character from Mrs Smith.)

Once simply waiting to glimpse her beloved, by now she is active in pursuit: her 'elegant' social self with its high-bred sense of good manners is no longer in charge and desire has taken over. Paradoxically, it allows more control of the body: when she and Wentworth meet in Bath, his rather than her body reacts with blushes. Where he becomes unsure of Anne once he feels renewed affection, Anne harbours no doubts of her returning power over him – unlike previous heroines she is no ingénue in courtship. Loving deeply, she never judges or blames Wentworth, who – presumably in striking contrast to his behaviour at sea – walks away from situations he cannot easily control: from Anne in 1806, from his sister when they start to discuss female roles, and, most arrogantly, from Louisa.

Anne shares with Wentworth a mordant humour, which both feel they should contain. She catches him suppressing a contemptuous smile when he thinks of the unlovable Dick Musgrove in Uppercross, for whom his mother is emitting 'fat sighings'. This mockery of the obese is notorious from an author who elsewhere stresses the absurdity of associating beauty with moral worth.[22] It seems to tie the narrator, Anne, and Wentworth to Sir Walter and his snobbish physical judging. However, it is also worth considering that this narrative aside, which has appalled so many of her critics, is probably close to Jane Austen's own wicked humour: her letters are shot through with similar sarcasm, whether it be a simple snide remark on physical shortcomings such as a Mrs Blount's 'broad face', 'pink Husband, & fat neck', or an unsentimental joke on poor Mrs Hall, who suffered a miscarriage after a fright – 'she happened unawares to look at her husband', *L*, pp. 17, 61). Wentworth again allows 'disdain in his eye' when he receives a card from Elizabeth Elliot, then checks the 'contempt in his mouth' as Mary remarks on the condescension of the act. Anne, too, smiles with contempt when she sees the littleness of which Elizabeth is proud in Bath, and she is scathing about the aristocratic Dalrymples. She approves of people making much of what they have, as the Harvilles and Mrs Smith do, but mocks the absurdity of showy people in reduced circumstances. As the problem of inviting the Musgroves for dinner makes plain, Elizabeth *does* know the difference between Kellynch Hall and a few rooms in Bath – 'she could not bear to have the difference of style, the reduction of servants, which a dinner must betray, witnessed'. She is aware she is growing older for she averts her eyes from the *Baronetage*, which notes her age and spinsterhood, while her father avoids Lady Russell by day since her crow's-foot wrinkles remind him of his own age. But Anne has no sympathy for sister or father. From such attitudes it seems that her peripheral position in the family may be as much from her own recoil as from exclusion.

Mrs Smith declares that 'even the smooth surface of family-union seems worth preserving though there may be nothing durable beneath'. In the early part of the novel Anne agrees, as she copes with her relations through moderate flattery and self-repressing tact. Although she baulks at telling her father and sister that the Kellynch tenants miss them, she gives Henrietta the supportive replies about her fiancé she knows she wants and keeps up a correspondence with Elizabeth. She is silent when she sees a parallel between Mrs Smith and Mrs Clay. (It is left to the reader to notice a similar parallel between Mrs Clay and herself in the way both keep others in countenance.) In this social activity she plays a traditional familial role, as she does when she looks after her sick nephew and finds her sister a dry place to sit when out of doors. The servile actions become so habitual that, even when she has emotionally shifted in the second half of the book in Bath, on meeting her relatives, the Musgroves, she 'naturally fell into all her wonted ways of attention and assistance'.

And yet, although she has decided to 'go with the others', Anne is in fact even more appalled at her family than Elizabeth Bennet was at hers, and her father commands noticeably less respect from her than the flawed patriarchs of *Mansfield Park* and *Emma*. She is clear that, whatever she had properly accepted as a young girl, she now thinks passion, sexual passion, more important than anything else in her life, certainly more than security, rank, and kinship. In this she has proceeded contrarily to that other woman of twenty-seven, Charlotte Lucas, who found the years confirming her lack of romance.

Anne's withdrawal from social service is expressed through the power of her inner world. In the *Juvenilia* and her early novels, Austen had mocked sentimental writing developed from Richardson's theatrical prose by women such as Mary Hays in *Memoirs of Emma Courtney* (1796) and used more recently by Burney in her much criticised final novel *The Wanderer* (1814); despite differing political opinions, both authors had tried to catch the turmoil of a woman's inner response to her confined and repressed existence through deploying a nervous, flamboyant typography and broken, agitated syntax. Austen had begun occasionally to develop this in more restrained form in *Mansfield Park* and *Emma*. Here, she goes farther: as the heroine had learnt romance as she grew older, so her creator has, it seems, come fully to romantic prose in her late novel, and Anne's first encounter with Wentworth is displayed in the broken syntax and repetition which reveal the faltering of ordinary response and control: 'a bow, a curtsey passed; she heard his voice – he talked to Mary, said all that was right; said something to the Miss Musgroves, enough to mark an easy footing: the room seemed full, full of persons and voices'.[23]

The external world which had such reality in *Emma* where 'nothing' did not serve does not always serve Anne Elliot. Beside the contented picture of village life Emma observes from Ford's door can be put Anne's bustling drive 'through the long course of streets from the Old Bridge to Camden-place, amidst the dash of other carriages, the heavy rumble of carts and drays, the bawling of newsmen, muffin-men and milk-men, and the ceaseless clink of pattens' (*P*, 2:2). Fastidious about noise, Anne blots out or condenses the world's cacophony when her inner life becomes too powerful here, and at the end, when she is 'heedless' of sauntering politicians and bustling housewives.

Sometimes the moments of absorption are close to the effect of the poet Wordsworth's famous 'spots of time' in 'Tintern Abbey' or *The Prelude*, instances of revelation that become central to human existence. At the same time, they develop a habit Austen had shown even in the earliest novels. In *Sense and Sensibility*, after her sister's painful encounter with her faithless lover, Elinor is lost in thought of her own beloved Edward: she forgets the letters on her lap and walks from the window to the fire and back receiving no warmth; when at the end Edward comes to claim her, he forgets the external world sufficiently to destroy Elinor's scissors and sheath. In *Persuasion*, such moments are more overwhelming, making the heroine dizzy and her surroundings a blur. When she spies Wentworth, 'for a few minutes she saw nothing before her. All was confusion.' When in the Octagon Room Wentworth speaks agitatedly of constancy concerning Fanny Harville and Captain Benwick ('A man does not recover from such a devotion of the heart to such a woman! – He ought not – he does not') she hears every word despite 'the almost ceaseless slam of the door, and ceaseless buzz of persons walking through' (*P*, 2:8). In the White Hart Inn, before the climactic scene of Wentworth's letter, she tries to listen to Mrs Croft speaking of long engagements while watching her lover when she can and musing on her past: 'Anne heard nothing distinctly; it was only a buzz of words in her ear, her mind was in confusion' (*P*, 2:11). When she holds the crucial letter, 'she began not to understand a word' anyone said; her response is so extreme that she appears sick; [24] the unimaginative Mrs Musgrove relates its effect to Louisa's fall. Even in her moment of realisation, when her knowledge of her own desires shoots through her like an arrow, or when she feels the pain of possible loss in her body, Emma never loses sight of her surroundings.

This blurring of inner and outer is informed by another conjunction: of pleasure and pain. When she first sees Wentworth redden at meeting her in Bath, Anne feels bewildered, then bewilderment gives way to 'agitation, pain, pleasure, a something between delight and misery'. Even as the wheel turns and fortune comes towards her, she is still in 'the happiness of such misery, or the misery of such happiness'. Through her years of depression and repression she had become, like Byron's passionate heroes, a connoisseur of pain, feeling it, stoking it, but hiding it inside: at the end her happiness is so extreme she needs to 'find an alloy in some momentary apprehension of its being impossible to last', and then to temper her 'high-wrought felicity' with serious meditation. Finally, the balance of pain and pleasure tilts towards pleasure: 'when pain is over, the remembrance of it often becomes a pleasure'. Anne grows 'steadfast and fearless in the thankfulness of her enjoyment'. This robust response of 'enjoyment' was very consciously created by Austen, who allows it to surge out of ordinary life and habit. In the first version of the novel's ending, she had medicalised it: Anne is awake all night, having to 'pay for the overplus of Bliss, by Headake & Fatigue'.

Loving longest

While Austen was composing *Persuasion*, Walter Scott's review of *Emma* appeared. In it he digressed to consider how few present instances there were of 'first attachments being brought to a happy conclusion'; modern youth was, he considered, now too worldly wise. Yet, 'after the pain of disappointment is past, those who survive . . . are neither less wise nor less worthy members of society for having felt, for a time, the influence of a passion which has been well qualified as the "tenderest, noblest and best"'.[25] This outburst on the need of a little romance in a man's life must have amused Jane Austen, halfway through writing *Persuasion* with its 'happy conclusion' of a 'first attachment'.

This comes about for Anne and Wentworth through the famous conversation in the White Hart Inn between the heroine and Captain Harville. Continuing the novel's gender debate, it ostensibly concerns men's and women's characters in love.[26] Through it Anne seizes the initiative with Wentworth and wrests the narrative from its bleak, even desolate trajectory of insecurity, age, and waste. Frequently she had lived in the internal world of the subjunctive: 'how eloquent could she have been' or she 'could have said much'; so it is appropriate that here she speaks aloud in the indicative rather than writing or gesturing, and that the story-telling Wentworth is silent as she finally, if obliquely, communicates with him. Her assertions are ideologically at odds with much of the gloomy common-sense of the book and do little to disrupt the quotidian life of selfishness and vanity it portrays; yet they profoundly stir most readers. The power of her rhetoric of personal self-sacrifice contrasts with the impotence of her earlier rhetorical interventions on behalf of the navy's national sacrifice.

Continuing a theme that has surfaced at intervals through the book, she begins the dialogue by denouncing literature as male and untrue: it is a duplicitous move for she is disallowing it as experience just before appealing most intensely to a literary aesthetic – for what else is her climactic statement of constancy beyond life and hope? She then argues that women are stationary in emotions because physically stationary:

> We cannot help ourselves. We live at home, quiet, confined, and our feelings prey upon us. You are forced on exertion. You have always a profession, pursuits, business of some sort or other to take you back into the world immediately, and continual occupation and change soon weaken impressions.   (*P*, 2:11)

Harville responds with the apostasy of the stationary Benwick. Anne takes another angle: 'If the change be not from outward circumstances, it must be from within; it must be nature.' Harville demurs, insisting that the virtue of constancy cannot be gendered or, if it is, must be to men's advantage: 'as our bodies are the strongest, so are our feelings'. He describes the 'glow' of 'soul' in the returning seaman. Anne responds:

> I believe you capable of everything great and good in your married lives. I believe you equal to every important exertion, and to every domestic forbearance, so long as – if I may be allowed the expression, so long as you have an object. I mean, while the woman you love lives, and lives for you. All the privilege I claim for my own sex (it is not a very enviable one, you need not covet it), is that of loving longest, when existence or when hope is gone.   (*P*, 2:11)

This operatic speech vibrates with the rhetoric that has been consciously repressed throughout the novel. (It's hard to imagine that its writing was an afterthought and not the germ of the novel.) Anne says no more than many men and women had said before her concerning the inhibited state of women in society, from the Romantic misogyny of Byron – 'man's love is of man's life a thing apart, / 'Tis woman's whole existence' – to Mary Hays's lament in *Emma Courtney* that social constraint results in debilitating romantic love written on the female 'mind in characters of blood'.[27] Here, the self-sacrificial stance gains beauty through its embedding in a whole life – and its use as part of seduction by (and of) a woman. The ordinary love of young Anne and Wentworth in 1806 depended on the boredom of the one and isolation of the other: the intervening years of suffering have turned it into 'romance'.

Through Anne Elliot's eloquence Austen avoids her usual retreat from female discourse in moments of high emotion. Here, rhetoric, eloquence, or literary style allow us a fantasy, undisturbed by irony, of following to its end what in life would be philosophically and even psychologically irrational. As David Hume remarked, 'Nothing is more capable of infusing any passion into the mind, than eloquence, by which objects are represented in their strongest and most lively colours' – whatever the melancholy of the content.[28] The narrator had observed that a 'second attachment [was] the only thoroughly natural, happy, and sufficient cure' for first love; here the heroine's contrary statement captures the hero and reader.[29] The rhetorical speech is 'apotropaic', that is it wards off what might have been and what still exists in the reader's mind, the wasted, longing life.

Unlike Captain Benwick, whom Harville castigates for *not* living up to the romantic ideal, and unlike Scott's pragmatic modern gentleman in the review, Anne has been faithful to the notion of a great single love, allowing 'all which this world could do for her' to depend on one man.[30] In *Sense and Sensibility* Elinor tells her sister, 'after all that is bewitching in the idea of a single and constant attachment, and all that can be said of one's happiness depending entirely on any particular person . . . it is not possible that it should be so' (*S&S*, 3:1). *Persuasion* both shows the destructive folly of romantic, self-sacrificial love, and reveals its supreme value.

Although the narrator has teasingly seen pretty 'musings of high-wrought love and eternal constancy' walking down the Bath streets, and although she bustles in with the usual sense of fictionality through her infamous questions, asking 'who can doubt of what followed?' the sardonic ending of the other novels is absent from *Persuasion*. There is none of the absurdity of the 'perfect felicity' of Catherine and Henry Tilney, the muted detail of learnt love in *Sense and Sensibility*, the sudden bathetic resolution of *Emma*. Only *Pride and Prejudice* implies such intensity of extra-familial feeling and then only on the man's side. *Persuasion* alone has intensity of both lovers and presents mature sexual love uncontaminated by glamorous possessions.[31]

Afterword

There is no complete and easy answer as to why Jane Austen, a novelist who enjoyed a modicum of success during her lifetime, nowadays has such a wide appeal, while the most popular writers of her period – those whom she herself admired – Samuel Richardson, Frances Burney, Maria Edgeworth, and Walter Scott, are rarely read for pleasure. It seems that Austen's fiction – like Sir Walter Elliot's face – has aged well 'amidst the wreck' of her contemporaries. I have suggested that her success is due to her unrivalled creation of plausible characters and their idiolects, her melding of emotional analysis and psychological acuity with social satire and comedy. Also, size may matter: Austen's minimalist narrative style distinguishes her from both her contemporaries and the great writers who followed her in the nineteenth century, the Brontës, George Eliot, Charles Dickens, and Henry James. She 'lop't & crop't so successfully' (*L*, p. 202) throughout much of her creative process until only a fast-paced narrative remained – the ramblings of Scott's colourful peasant folk may safely be skipped, as can the satirical spates of Burney's whimsical oddballs, but readers who mistake Miss Bates's compulsive chatter as equally immaterial to the plot will find themselves lacking pieces in the puzzle that is Jane Fairfax's secret engagement. And Austen's novels do not contain any of the tedious excursions characterising the fiction of her period: to omit 'long Chapter[s] – of sense', 'an Essay on Writing, a critique on Walter Scott, or the history of Buonaparte' (*L*, p. 203) was her conscious aesthetic decision – one which may have lost her critical appreciation among reviewers at the time but which has secured her popularity in a century when literary didacticism has fallen from fashion.

Austen's popularity may also be due to her 'limitation' – that recurring axiom in Austen criticism. Unlike the heroic tales of Scott, her fiction, while drawing on its social and historical moment, eschews explicit reference to the political revolutions of the eighteenth and early nineteenth century; it is not *anchored* within a specifically defined period. Even exterior detail is scarce. Readers follow the heroines of Burney's comedies into the dark alleyways of Vauxhall pleasure gardens and to sumptuous masquerades with a fairly clear notion of the material world in which they move; Austen's characters live in the same world but her audience is supplied with few markers (as it happens, the curious reader's desire for such frivolous information is only satisfied – and mocked – through the tedious inventories proffered by status-hungry Mr Collins). Mostly the social world of Austen's ballrooms and dining parties impinges on a reader's consciousness filtered through the heroine's emotions: the boredom, jealousies, and grievances, trivial or considerable, that are certain corollaries of human interaction – sentiments and situations which appear startlingly similar to those of the twenty-first century. 'We are more pleased with pictures of characters, which resemble such as are found in our own age or country', David Hume wrote in 'Of the Standard of Taste',[1] and Austen's novels appear to lend themselves to this semblance of 'timelessness' and continued relevance: despite moving within a miniaturist world peopled by '3 or 4 Families in a Country Village' (*L*, p. 275), all invariably genteel and mostly moneyed, her fiction succeeds in revealing what even a post-Freudian audience perceives as a truthful representation of human consciousness.

I have stated that Austen's narrators are frequently unforthcoming, grudgingly sharing their insight into character; when given, their judgement is rarely wholly reliable, coloured as it mostly is by the heroines' subjective perception. Perhaps it is this quality of Austen's writing that accounts for the widespread opinion that somehow her novels are more 'realistic' than those of her contemporaries. Austen's fictional world approximates real-life experience – the lack of absolute knowability, the necessarily futile, engagingly absurd attempts at wholly fathoming our own selves and others. By thus granting her characters a depth of human freedom, Austen forces us to become actively involved in the analysis of their psychology – and once this involvement in the fictional world has been triggered, it seems only plausible that the characters we have helped to shape in our minds strike us as 'real' and continue as part of our own mental landscapes.

Notes

Preface

1 Charlotte Brontë to W. S. Williams, 12 April 1850, *The Letters of Charlotte Brontë*, ed. Margaret Smith (Oxford: Clarendon Press, 2000), vol. 2, p. 383.
2 Ann Jessie Van Sant, *Eighteenth-Century Sensibility and the Novel. The Senses in Social Context* (Cambridge University Press, 1993), p. 53.
3 Laurence Sterne, *The Life and Opinions of Tristram Shandy* (1759–67), vol. 1, ch. 23.

1 Life and times

1 John Wiltshire, *Recreating Jane Austen* (Cambridge University Press, 2001), p. 17.
2 See Robert Clark and Gerry Dutton, 'Agriculture' in *Jane Austen in Context*, ed. Janet Todd (Cambridge University Press, 2005), pp. 185–93.
3 In *Jane Austen's 'Outlandish Cousin', the Life and Letters of Eliza de Feuillide* (London: British Library, 2002), Deirdre Le Faye traces the rumour of Eliza's illegitimacy to Mrs Strachey, wife of the secretary to the then Governor of Bengal, Lord Clive. Hancock never appears to have doubted his paternity, pp. 19–20.
4 See Penny Gay, *Jane Austen and the Theatre* (Cambridge University Press, 2002), pp. 4–6.
5 Le Faye, *Jane Austen's 'Outlandish Cousin'*, p. 155.
6 Virginia Woolf, *The Common Reader. First Series* (London: Hogarth Press, 1968), pp. 170–1.
7 The dating is disputed. Brian Southam in *Jane Austen's Literary Manuscripts*, new edition (London: Athlone Press, 2001), p. 147, thinks late 1793 or 1794; R. W. Chapman suggests 1805 in *Jane Austen, Facts and Problems* (Oxford: Clarendon Press, 1948) pp. 49–50; and, in her entry for Jane Austen in the *Oxford Dictionary of National Biography* (Oxford University Press, 2004), Marilyn Butler argues for a date around 1810.
8 Walter Scott, 'Review of *Emma*', *Quarterly Review* 14 (October, 1815 [March, 1816]), 188–201.
9 W. H. Auden, 'Letter to Lord Byron', *Collected Longer Poems* (New York: Random House, 1969), p. 41.

10 This extreme reaction was a late addition to family memoirs, appearing in William and Richard Arthur Austen-Leigh, *Jane Austen: Her Life and Letters. A Family Record* (London, 1913), pp. 155–6.

11 Harold Perkin, *The Origins of Modern English Society*, second edition (London: Routledge, 2002), p. 255.

12 Caroline Austen, *My Aunt Jane Austen: A Memoir* (Alton: Jane Austen Society, 1952), p. 5.

13 Kathryn Sutherland, 'Chronology of Composition' in *Jane Austen in Context*, pp. 12–22.

14 In *Memoir*, pp. 133–4, James Edward Austen-Leigh points out that the first memory must be inaccurate since it would have to be based on knowledge of Austen as 'a little girl'.

15 Peter Garside, 'The English Novel in the Romantic Era' in *The English Novel 1770–1829: A Bibliographical Survey of Prose Fiction Published in the British Isles*, ed. Garside, James Raven, and Rainer Schöwerling (Oxford University Press, 2000), vol. 2, p. 75.

16 See Sutherland, 'Chronology of Composition', p. 21.

17 For a discussion of Jane Austen's symptoms during her fatal illness see Claire Tomalin, *Jane Austen. A Life* (London: Penguin Books, 1998), pp. 287–8, and *FR*, p. 236.

18 Henry Austen, 'Biographical Notice' in *Memoir*.

19 *Jane Austen: Collected Poems and Verse of the Austen Family*, ed. David Selwyn (Manchester: Carcanet Press, 1996), p. 17.

20 *The Examiner*, 12 March 1815, 162–3.

21 Margaret Oliphant, 'Miss Austen and Miss Mitford', *Blackwood's Edinburgh Magazine* 107: 653 (March 1870), 294.

22 However, she did described the government as 'pitiful' and 'mean' in 'On Sir Home Popham's sentence – April 1807', *Jane Austen: Collected Poems*, p. 7.

23 For a full discussion see Peter Knox-Shaw, *Jane Austen and the Enlightenment* (Cambridge University Press, 2004) and his entry 'Philosophy' in *Jane Austen in Context*, pp. 346–56.

2 The literary context

1 'But man, whom Nature form'd of milder clay, / With every kind emotion in his heart, / And taught alone to weep.' James Thomson, *The Seasons*, 'Spring', lines 350–2.

2 Mary Lascelles, *Jane Austen and her Art* (Oxford: Clarendon Press, 1939), pp. 107–8.

3 In her letter of 1796 Jane Austen mocks the plot of *Camilla* when she asks Cassandra to tell a friend that she hopes when she is 'attached to a young Man, some *respectable* Dr. Marchmont may keep them apart for five volumes' (*L*, p. 9).

4 George Gordon, Lord Byron, *Don Juan* (1818) canto I, stanza xvi.

5 Richard Whately, *Quarterly Review* 24 (October and January 1821), 367.

6 Mary Hays, *Letters and Essays* (London, 1793), p. 20. Mary Wollstonecraft, *A Vindication of the Rights of Woman, The Works of Mary Wollstonecraft*, ed. Janet Todd and Marilyn Butler (London: Pickering & Chatto, 1989), vol. 5, p. 75.

7 David Hume, 'Of the Rise and Progress of the Arts and Sciences' in *Essays and Treatises on Several Subjects* (London, 1758), p. 71.

8 Samuel Johnson, *The Rambler*, ed. W. J. Bate and A. B. Strauss, *The Yale Edition of the Works of Samuel Johnson* (New Haven: Yale University Press, 1969), no. 60, vol. 3, pp. 318–19.

9 They are surrounded by what E. M. Forster called 'flat' characters who, treated satirically, signify their presence in predictable eccentricities and repeated gestures. Yet even these may have sudden depth, e.g. when in *P&P* the unctuous Mr Collins's uncertain sense of self is explained by his 'illiterate' and overbearing father and faith in conduct books.

10 Deidre Shauna Lynch, *The Economy of Character. Novels, Market, Culture and the Business of Inner Meaning* (University of Chicago Press, 1998), p. 10.

11 Austen becomes Jerome J. McGann's prime example of a woman writing in the Romantic period but not being a Romantic writer, so departing from the 'dominant ideological commitments' of her age, *The Romantic Ideology. A Critical Investigation* (University of Chicago Press, 1983), p. 19. In contrast Clifford Siskin argues that Austen contributes to the Romantic ideology by joining the inward turn associated with Romanticism, *The Historicity of Romantic Discourse* (Oxford University Press, 1988), pp. 125–47.

12 William Gilpin had pointed out that 'a few strokes of the pencil' are better than 'a volume of the most laboured description', *Observations, Relative chiefly to Picturesque Beauty, made in the Year 1772, on Several Parts of England; Particularly the Mountains, and Lakes of Cumberland, and Westmoreland* (1786), p. xxiii; he thought exact imitation of less value than plausibility.

13 Julia Kavanagh, *English Women of Letters. Biographical Sketches* (Leipzig: Bernhard Tauchnitz, 1862), p. 257.

14 This play might have influenced *Pride and Prejudice*'s depiction of haughty Darcy's attraction to pert Elizabeth, see Gay, *Jane Austen and the Theatre*, pp. 73–4.

15 John A. Dussinger, *In the Pride of the Moment: Encounters in Jane Austen's World* (Columbus: Ohio State University Press, 1990), p. 176.

16 *The Journal of Sir Walter Scott*, ed. W. E. K. Anderson (Oxford: Clarendon Press, 1972), entry for 14 March 1826, p. 114.

17 James Thompson, *Between Self and World. The Novels of Jane Austen* (University Park: Pennsylvania State University Press, 1988), p. 101.

18 Ralph Waldo Emerson, *Journals of Ralph Waldo Emerson*, ed. Edward Waldo Emerson and Waldo Emerson Forbes (Boston: Houghton Mifflin, 1909), p. 336; Mark Twain, *Following the Equator: A Journey around the World* (Hartford, CT: The American Publishing Company, 1897), p. 615; Ezra Pound, review of Robert Frost's *North of Boston, Poetry*, December 1914.

19 F. R. Leavis, *The Great Tradition* (London: Chatto & Windus, 1948), p. 7; Reginald Farrer, 'Jane Austen, *ob.* July 18, 1817', *Quarterly Review* 228: 452 (July and October 1917), 1–30; D. W. Harding, 'Regulated Hatred: an Aspect of the Work of Jane Austen', *Scrutiny. A Quarterly Review* 8:4 (1940), 346–62; Marvin Mudrick, *Jane Austen: Irony as Defense and Discovery* (Princeton University Press, 1952); Ian Watt, *The Rise of the Novel* (Chatto & Windus, 1957), pp. 296–7.

20 Sandra M. Gilbert and Susan Gubar, *The Madwoman in the Attic. The Woman Writer and the Nineteenth-Century Literary Imagination* (New Haven and London: Yale University Press, 1979), p. 169.

21 Edmund Burke, *Reflections on the Revolution in France* (London: Penguin Classics, 1986), pp. 121, 135, 194.

22 For contrary or modified interpretations see Claudia L. Johnson, who argued that Austen focused 'on the discourse rather than the representation of politics' and defended 'a progressive middle ground that had been eaten away by the polarizing polemics born of the 1790s', *Jane Austen. Women, Politics and the Novel* (Chicago University Press, 1988), p. 27; Nancy Armstrong, who connected Austen with a middle-class aristocracy, *Desire and Domestic Fiction: A Political History of the Novel* (Oxford University Press, 1987); Jan Fergus, who thought Austen's political sympathies could be 'fundamentally conservative' while her mind was 'critical and her vision ironic', *Jane Austen: A Literary Life* (Basingstoke and London: Macmillan, 1991), p. 67.

23 Raymond Williams, *The Country and the City*, new edition (London: Chatto & Windus, 1973), pp. 112–19.

24 Eve Kosofsky Sedgwick, 'Jane Austen and the Masturbating Girl', *Critical Inquiry* 17 (Summer 1991), 818–37; Claudia L. Johnson, *Equivocal Beings: Politics, Gender and Sentimentality in the 1790s: Wollstonecraft, Radcliffe, Burney, Austen* (University of Chicago Press, 1995).

3 *Northanger Abbey*

1 Medical writers like Alexander Crichton (in *An Inquiry into the Nature and Origin of Mental Derangement*, 1798) and novelists were much concerned with the effects of representation. In *Ormond* (1817) Maria Edgeworth portrays a young man unable to differentiate between life and art – a novel 'appeared no fiction, while he was reading it', *Tales and Novels*, vol. 9, p. 294.

2 Johnson, *The Rambler, Yale Edition*, no. 4, vol. 3, p. 22.

3 The date of drafting is give in Cassandra's memorandum, see *FR*, p. 259.

4 James Fordyce, *The Character and Conduct of the Female Sex* (1776), p. 48.

5 Entry between December 1808 and January 1809, *The Notebooks of Samuel Taylor Coleridge* (London: Routledge, 2002), vol. 3, 3449 14.24. Although Austen mocks aspects of the gothic, the moderation of her response can be gauged in comparison

with the single-minded burlesque of Eaton Stannard Barrett's *The Heroine, or Adventures of a Fair Romance Reader* (1813), where the fiction-addled girl ends up in a lunatic asylum.

6 Johnson, *The Rambler, Yale Edition*, no. 208, vol. 5, pp. 318–19.

7 Gilpin, *Essay Upon Prints* (1768), p. 2. Gilpin was writing on landscape from the 1740s but he achieved most fame in the 1780s, beginning with *Observations on the River Wye* (1782).

8 Gilpin, *Observations, Relative chiefly to Picturesque Beauty*, vol. 1, p. 81.

9 The social and political significance of the picturesque is also suggested when Henry moves from forests, enclosure, land ownership, and politics to silence. The point is only lightly made, however, and there is little evidence that Henry is being presented as a reformer any more than a serious clergyman.

10 Gerald Prince, 'Introduction to the Study of the Narratee', *Reader-Response Criticism: From Formalism to Post-Structuralism*, ed. Jane P. Tompkins (Baltimore: Johns Hopkins University Press, 1980), pp. 7–25.

11 Frances Burney, 'Preface' to *Evelina*, ed. Margaret Anne Doody (London: Penguin Books, 1994), p. 8; Maria Edgeworth, 'Advertisement' to *Belinda*, ed. Kathryn J. Kirkpatrick (Oxford University Press, 1994), p. 3.

4 Sense and Sensibility

1 'The story may be thought trifling by the readers of novels, who are insatiable after *something new*', *Critical Review, series the fourth*, 1:2 (February 1812), 149.

2 Hume, 'The Sceptic', *Essays and Treatises*, p. 105.

3 Tony Tanner, *Jane Austen* (Houndmills: Macmillan, 1986), p. 90.

4 Hume, 'Of the Delicacy of Taste and Passion', *Essays and Treatises*, p. 3.

5 Structurally Brandon's long story is clumsy, a faint echo of the recitations interrupting the plot of sentimental novels which the young Jane Austen burlesqued.

6 Marvin Mudrick, *Irony as Defense*, pp. 91–3.

7 David Hume, *A Treatise of Human Nature, being an Attempt to Introduce the Experimental Method of Reasoning into Moral Subjects*, (London, 1739–40), vol. 2, p. 248.

8 See Janet Todd, *Mary Wollstonecraft, a Revolutionary Life* (London: Weidenfeld & Nicolson, 2000), pp. 371–2.

9 Mary Wollstonecraft and William Godwin, *A Short Residence in Sweden and Memoirs of the Author of 'The Rights of Woman'* (London: Penguin Classics, 1987), ch. 8; *The Collected Letters of Mary Wollstonecraft* (London: Penguin Books, 2004), p. 371.

5 Pride and Prejudice

1 In *Jane Austen and the Fiction of Culture: An Essay on the Narration of Social Realities* (Lanham, MD: Rowman & Littlefield, 1999), Richard Handler and Daniel Segal

call the opening 'a parody of an aphorism – a somewhat dubious statement that undercuts itself through excessive certainty, thereby becoming what Bakhtin terms "double languaged"' (p. 116).

2 Lionel Trilling sees the marriage of Elizabeth and Darcy as a reconciliation of male 'formal rhetoric, traditional and rigorous' and 'female vivacity', *Opposing Self. Nine Essays in Criticism* (London: Secker and Warburg, 1955), p. 222, while Tanner, *Jane Austen*, p. 141, calls it a metaphor for a union of 'energy and boundaries'. Some feminist critics stress the deflating fate of the heroine in an unequal marriage: see, for example, Karen Newman, 'Can This Marriage Be Saved: Jane Austen Makes Sense of an Ending', *ELH* 50:4 (1983), 704–5, and Mary Poovey, who remarked that the novel 'legitimises the reader's romantic wishes by humbling the heroine's vanity', *The Proper Lady and the Woman Writer* (University of Chicago Press, 1984), p. 201.

3 Although R. W. Chapman noted that its action fits well with the calendar of 1811–12, its tone is of the 1790s and the early war years rather than the Regency, 'Chronology of *Pride and Prejudice*' in *Pride and Prejudice*, ed. Chapman, new edition (Oxford University Press, 1988), p. 401.

4 The nationalistic English aspect of this character will be clearer in *Emma* in Mr Knightley.

5 Burke, *Reflections*, p. 183.

6 Knox-Shaw points out that Elizabeth here echoes Adam Smith, who said that high self-esteem in others, even when well founded, 'mortifies our own', 'Philosophy', *Jane Austen in Context*, p. 353.

7 Hume, 'Of Qualities Useful to Ourselves', *Essays and Treatises*, p. 447.

8 Franco Moretti, *Way of the World: The Bildungsroman in European Culture* (London: Verso, 1987), pp. 36–7.

9 Adela Pinch, *Strange Fits of Passion. Epistemologies of Emotion. Hume to Austen* (Stanford University Press, 1996), p. 38.

10 Even Austen's favourite poet Cowper in *The Task*, bk 1 'The Sofa', lines 215–17, proposed that ladies stay in when the ground is wet: 'When Winter soaks the fields, and female feet . . . are best at home'.

11 Edward Neill in *The Politics of Jane Austen* (London: Macmillan, 1999), p. 52, goes so far as to claim that Elizabeth capitulates in the second part of the book and that the relationship is a 'master–slave' one.

6 *Mansfield Park*

1 Farrer, 'Jane Austen, *ob.* July 18, 1817', 20.

2 Tanner, *Jane Austen*, p. 171.

3 C. W. Pasley, *Essay on the Military Policy and Institutions of the British Empire*, 3rd edition (London, 1811), p. 231.

4 Edward Said, *Culture and Imperialism* (London: Chatto & Windus, 1993). The novel's title has been connected with Lord Mansfield, who in 1772 gave the judgment preventing slavery on English soil. Abolition was a special cause of Jane Austen's admired Thomas Clarkson and Sir Thomas's silence most likely obscures the liberal views that almost everyone in Austen's immediate circle held, while they benefited from slavery; Austen's brother Francis was an outspoken opponent of slavery and her father was trustee of a plantation in Antigua.

5 One might argue that Fanny learns from Lady Bertram's achievement since she, too, marries above her 'equitable claim' through the 'most enduring claims' of 'helplessness'.

6 'To Penshurst', *Ben Jonson. The Complete Poems*, ed. George Parfitt (London: Penguin, 1975), p. 97, lines 95–6.

7 In keeping with its tastefully improved status, Pemberley had a more modern and therefore hidden ha-ha instead of an iron gate.

8 Samuel Johnson, *The Idler and The Adventurer*, ed. W. J. Bate, John M. Bullitt, L. F. Powell *The Yale Edition of the Works of Samuel Johnson* (New Haven: Yale University Press, 1963), no. 74, vol. 2, p. 232.

9 Lionel Trilling, 'Mansfield Park' in *Jane Austen. A Collection of Critical Essays*, ed. Ian Watt (Englewood Cliffs, NJ: Prentice-Hall, 1966), p. 137.

10 Frequent in aristocratic circles in the eighteenth century, cousin marriage was not incest according to the Church of England.

11 The Prince Regent's librarian, James Stanier Clarke, amused Austen by recommending that she 'delineate in some future Work the Habits of Life and Character and enthusiasm of a Clergyman' (*L*, p. 296); *Mansfield Park* went some way towards this, although Austen avoided the evangelical tone which Clark's emphasis on 'enthusiasm' suggests.

12 Compare 'Catharine, or the Bower', where the comically strict aunt tells the heroine: 'the welfare of every Nation depends upon the virtue of it's individuals, and any one who offends in so gross a manner against decorum and propriety is certainly hastening it's ruin'.

13 *Two Letters Addressed to A Member of the Present Parliament, on the Proposals for Peace with the Regicide Directory of France by the Right Honourable Edmund Burke*, second edition (London, 1796), p. 126.

14 Michael Giffin, *Jane Austen and Religion: Salvation and Society in Georgian England* (Basingstoke: Palgrave, 2002), pp. 126 and 136.

15 Hannah More, *An Estimate of the Religion of the Fashionable World* (1791), p. 15.

16 Mary's manners falter towards the novel's close, e.g. her crass letter to Fanny speculating on Tom's death and Edmund's elevation. The letter seems a flaw in the book but may illustrate her increasing desire to have Edmund in the worldly mould she wants.

17 Jane West, *Letters to a Young Lady in which the Duties and Character of Women are Considered* (London, 1806), vol. 2, pp. 484–5.

18 Trilling, *Opposing Self*, p. 212.

19 John Wiltshire, introduction to Jane Austen, *Mansfield Park* (Cambridge University Press, 2005), p. lxxvii.

20 Significantly the next chapter opens with the narrator informing us that Tom and Maria *do* triumph because they, like Fanny, understand Edmund's amorous motives – he, the future parson, has lost 'his moral elevation'. The response does not make Fanny appear less mean-spirited but it complicates the moral issue.

21 Whately, pp. 366–7. Susan Morgan and Susan Kneedler observe that *Mansfield Park* 'imagines love and passion as a friendly relation' with 'forms of affection that are both more loving and more personal than the codes of romantic love', 'Austen's Sexual Politics', *Persuasions* 12 (1990), p. 21, while Anne K. Mellor argues that Fanny should be read as 'a slave . . . "chained" in a marriage with Edmund, a marriage she has been manipulated into seeing as desirable', 'Directions in Austen Criticism' in *Re-Drawing Austen: Picturesque Travels in Austenland*, ed. Beatrice Battaglia and Diego Saglia (Naples: Liguori, 2004), p. 327.

7 *Emma*

1 Like *Pride and Prejudice, Emma* has one of Austen's most famous, abrupt openings: 'Emma Woodhouse, handsome, clever and rich, with a comfortable home and happy disposition, seemed to unite some of the best blessings of existence.' Only the 'seemed' suggests the narrator winking at the reader.

2 Trilling remarked: 'In *Emma* the heroine is made to stand at bay to our adverse judgement through virtually the whole novel, but we are never permitted to close in for the kill – some unnamed quality in the girl, some trait of vivacity or will, erects itself into a moral principle, at least a vital principle, and frustrates our moral blood-lust', *Jane Austen*, ed. Ian Watt, p. 125.

3 See Richard Cronin's introduction to Jane Austen, *Emma* (Cambridge University Press, 2005), pp. xlix–lii.

4 Johnson, *The History of Rasselas, Prince of Abissinia . . . Cooke's edition* (London, 1800), p. 53.

5 Catherine Talbot, *Essays on Various Subjects*, second edition (1772), vol. 1, pp. 25 and 161.

6 Fabricating a past is usually associated with rising capitalism in a nation; it may do so also in an individual.

7 Mudrick, *Irony as Defense*, pp. 190, 192 and 203.

8 In *Sanditon*, Charlotte sees Clara Brereton in much the same light. In her eagerness for Mr Elton to witness Harriet visiting the poor, Emma reveals herself as a reader of More's *Cœlebs*, which describes the seductive effect on the hero of the heroine's benevolence.

9 Richard Jenkyns sees Mr Woodhouse as the villain of the tale, a kind of octopus whose tentacles draw everyone to him and who tries to destroy everyone's pleasure: his passivity is 'aggressive and rapacious' and he is 'a bloodsucker, fastened upon

his daughter's flesh', *A Fine Brush on Ivory: An Appreciation of Jane Austen* (Oxford University Press, 2004), pp. 161–4.

10 Thomas Trotter, *A View of the Nervous Temperament*, second edition (London, 1807) p. 251.

11 William Gilpin, *Observations on the Western Parts of England, Relative Chiefly to Picturesque Beauty* (1798), p. 27.

12 Harding argues that the novel insists both on the reader's recognition of the evil impulses within society and on the need to contain and reconcile; in this reading a wrong act and a rude one are the same, 'Regulated Hatred', pp. 349–52.

13 Susan J. Wolfson, 'Boxing Emma; or the Reader's Dilemma at the Box Hill Games' in *Re-Reading Box Hill: Reading the Practice of Reading Everyday Life*, ed. William Galperin (College Park, MD: University of Maryland, 2000), no pagination.

14 Dussinger, *Pride of the Moment*, p. 113.

15 Tanner, *Jane Austen*, pp. 176–207. Beth Fowkes Tobin agreed that 'in linking Mr Knightley's gentlemanly virtues with his owning land, and Emma's moral inadequacies with her money and lack of property, Austen, acting as an apologist for the landed classes, was defending the "paternal system of government"', 'The Moral and Political Economy of Property in Austen's *Emma*', *Eighteenth-Century Fiction* 1:2 (1990), 229.

16 In his *Rural Oeconomy: Or, Essays on the Practical Parts of Husbandry* (1770) Young also observed that many professionals had turned farmer, pp. 174 and 177.

17 Tom Paine, *Rights of Man* (Harmondsworth: Penguin Classics, 1985), p. 227.

18 Burke, *Reflections*, p. 120.

19 A. Walton Litz, *Jane Austen: A Study of Her Artistic Development* (London: Chatto & Windus, 1965), p. 148. Alistair M. Duckworth writes that he 'remains the normative and exemplary figure he has traditionally been considered', *The Improvement of The Estate* (Baltimore: Johns Hopkins University Press, 1971), p. 148.

20 The description draws on picturesque depictions but is not primarily 'picturesque', the vogue for which had been waning since its hey-day of the 1790s.

21 Mr Knightley uses French imported words to describe what he disapproves: 'There is one thing, Emma, which a man can always do, if he chooses, and that is, his duty; not by manoeuvring and finessing, but by vigour and resolution'; see also Gay, *Jane Austen and the Theatre*, pp. 136 and 143.

22 Claudia L. Johnson has argued that, unlike in other novels of the time where heroines are either proved worthy of the hero by being meek, or are the poor victims of evil husbands, fathers, or lovers, Emma does not think of herself as 'an incomplete or contingent being'. The novel accepts a hierarchical society 'not because it is a sacred dictate of patriarchy . . . but rather because within its parameters class can actually supersede sex', *Jane Austen*, pp. 124 and 127.

23 Richard Cronin notes the prevalence of this trope in eighteenth-century fiction, especially Richardson's *Sir Charles Grandison* and more recently Elizabeth Inchbald's *A Simple Story* (1791) and Mary Brunton's *Self-Control* (1811), see his introduction to *Emma*, pp. xlviii–xlix.

8 *Persuasion*

1 Letter of 21 February 1818 in *A Memoir of Maria Edgeworth with A Selection from her Letters* (1867), vol. 2, pp. 5–6.

2 *Bamford's Passages in the Life of a Radical*, ed. Henry Dunckley (London, 1893), vol. 2, p. 11.

3 Nina Auerbach, 'O Brave New World: Evolution and Revolution in *Persuasion*', *ELH* 39:1 (1972), 117.

4 In an earlier version, instead of 'importance', Austen wrote 'renown', which the navy rather lacked at this time.

5 Reproduced in Margarette Lincoln, *Representing the Royal Navy* (London: Ashgate, 2002), plate 15. Several such caricatures were produced, working on nostalgia for the more manly and vigorous service of the past.

6 In *Mansfield Park*, Edmund calls the navy a 'noble profession' while Mary Crawford states it is 'well . . . if it makes the fortune'. Edgeworth calls officers primarily concerned with prize money 'calculating pirates', *Manoeuvring*, ch. 8. Although in 1814 good harvests and renewed import of grain impinged on landowners, making them less prosperous than in earlier years, and although Shepherd remarks that many are renting out their houses, the novel's emphasis is on Sir Walter and Elizabeth's particular extravagance and ill-management.

7 The estimated war dead is 200,000, the bulk of these being soldiers. Although many died from disease at sea, relatively few naval men died in battle.

8 John Wiltshire, *Jane Austen and the Body: 'The Picture of Health'* (Cambridge University Press, 1992), pp. 155–96.

9 Mary's anxiety was unfounded since, after 1815, the navy did extremely poorly in attracting baronetcies.

10 R. L. Edgeworth, *Essays on Professional Education* (London, 1809), p. 116.

11 Charles Rzepka's reading of *Persuasion* in 'Making it in a Brave New World: Marriage, Profession and Anti-Romantic *Ekstasis* in Austen's *Persuasion*', *Studies in the Novel* 26:2 (Summer 1994), 99–120, is a corrective to utopian feminist ones such as those of Gilbert and Gubar and Auerbach. But I cannot go quite as far as his counter argument that here marriage is a statement of conservative and evangelical ideals of domestic economy and feminine nurturing.

12 At the same time it may refer to the huge taxation for war which the nation must pay in peace.

13 The cruel effect on the body of life at sea was most graphically described in *Roderick Random* (1748) by the foremost maritime fictionist of the eighteenth century Tobias Smollett, who based his portrayal of the wounded, mutilated, torn, and diseased bodies of seamen on his own period as a ship's surgeon in the 1740s.

14 Such depictions will become common in the later nineteenth-century novel, for example in Charlotte Brontë's *Villette* (1853).

15 Alexander Crichton, *An Inquiry into the Nature and Origin of Mental Derangement* (1798), vol. 2, p. 65.

16 In 'Mourning and Melancholia in *Persuasion*', Elizabeth Dalton argued that Anne's resistance to Wentworth on his return exemplifies Freud's notion of 'introjection' of the lost object into the ego, 'where a sort of phantasmal relationship is maintained through suffering', *Partisan Review* 62 (Winter 1995), 50–1.

17 In the earlier version of the last chapters the physical contact climaxes when their two hands touch; in the later version it culminates in Anne sitting on the seat which Wentworth has just vacated.

18 Trotter, *Nervous Temperament*, pp. 49–59; see also R. Thomas, *The Modern Practice of Physic*, fifth edition (1817), p. 327.

19 Trotter, *Nervous Temperament*, p. xi.

20 Charlotte Smith, 'Written at the Close of Spring', *The Poems of Charlotte Smith*, ed. Stuart Curran (Oxford University Press, 1993), p. 14, lines 12–14. The imagery of renewed vegetation contrasting with dead humanity also informs the political poetry of Waterloo which Austen was reading at this time.

21 Historically the farmer is looking towards the spring of 1816, which, because of the eruption of Mount Tabora, was one of the worst and wettest on record.

22 Mudrick observes that the sneering description is followed by a 'bland apology' stating that fat people simply look ridiculous, *Irony as Defense*, p. 212; Wiltshire describes the paragraph as 'defensive floundering' which tries to read the body as a decypherable text, an attempt which the rest of the book repudiates, *Jane Austen and the Body*, p. 195.

23 Reginald Farrer wrote of this passage that the 'little flutter' of the repeated adjective here is all that is needed to leave 'the sensitised reader' fairly 'staggering in the gale of Anne's emotions', *Quarterly Review*, p. 7. Judging from Austen's manuscript of chapters of *Persuasion* she herself used many dashes in her text; compositors seemed more willing to reproduce these in the 1790s than in the 1810s.

24 Adela Pinch points out that the narrator uses locutions like 'Anne found herself' in a carriage or addressed by Wentworth, so stressing her self-absorption, *Strange Fits of Passion*, p. 152.

25 Although in the issue for October 1815, pp. 188–201, the review in fact appeared in March 1816.

26 According to James Edward Austen-Leigh, Jane Austen thought the first version of her final chapters without the conversation on love 'tame and flat'. She wanted to produce 'something better' and 'retired to rest in very low spirits'. Next morning 'the sense of power revived; and imagination resumed its course' and she rewrote. 'Perhaps it may be thought that she has seldom written anything more brilliant', he observed, *Memoir*, p. 125.

27 Byron, canto 1, stanza 194 of *Don Juan*; Mary Hays, *Emma Courtney*, vol. 1, p. 2. See also Peter Melville Logan, *Nerves and Narratives: A Cultural History of Hysteria in Nineteenth-Century British Prose* (Berkeley: University of California Press, 1997), p. 67.

28 Hume, *Treatise of Human Nature*, vol. 2, p. 268.

29 Not all critics are impressed with this rhetorical speech. Dussinger writes, 'No matter how climactic, this scene is too deliberately staged with podium and props to render the quintessential "language of real feeling"', *Pride of the Moment*, p. 172, while Miller deplores the 'inevitable litany of tributes "Moving, affecting, touching, poignant"' to describe a novel which he sees as 'the great sentimental favorite in the Austen canon and, not coincidentally, the great false step of Austen Style', *Jane Austen, or The Secret of Style* (Princeton University Press, 2003), pp. 75 and 68. Perhaps it is a gender matter, for I have come across few women who have not been 'moved'.

30 There was much discussion in late eighteenth-century novels concerning women's love and the value of first and second attachments.

31 Fittingly, Rudyard Kipling awarded Wentworth in the guise of a 'Hampshire gentleman' to Jane Austen herself in his comic poem 'Jane's Marriage' which he appended to his story 'The Janeites' in *Debits and Credits* (London, 1926), p. 176.

Afterword

1 Hume, 'Of the Standard of Taste', *Essays and Treatises*, p. 144.

Further reading

Armstrong, Nancy. *Desire and Domestic Fiction: A Political History of the Novel*. Oxford University Press, 1987.

Auerbach, Nina. 'O Brave New World: Evolution and Revolution in *Persuasion*', *ELH* 39:1 (1972), 112–28.

Butler, Marilyn. *Jane Austen and the War of Ideas*. Oxford: Clarendon Press, 1975.

Deresiewicz, William. *Jane Austen and the Romantic Poets*. New York: Columbia University Press, 2004.

Duckworth, Alistair M. *The Improvement of the Estate: A Study of Jane Austen's Novels*. Baltimore and London: Johns Hopkins University Press, 1971.

Dussinger, John A. *In the Pride of the Moment: Encounters in Jane Austen's World*. Columbus: Ohio State University Press, 1990.

Fergus, Jan. *Jane Austen: A Literary Life*. Basingstoke and London: Macmillan, 1991.

Galperin, William H. *The Historical Austen*. Philadelphia: Pennsylvania University Press, 2003.

Gard, Roger. *Jane Austen's Novels: The Art of Clarity*. New Haven: Yale University Press, 1992.

Gay, Penny. *Jane Austen and the Theatre*. Cambridge University Press, 2002.

Gilbert, Sandra M. and Susan Gubar. *The Madwoman in the Attic. The Woman Writer and the Nineteenth-Century Literary Imagination*. New Haven and London: Yale University Press, 1979.

Gilson, David, *A Bibliography of Jane Austen*. Oxford: Clarendon Press, 1982, repr. St Paul's Bibliographies, Winchester and Oak Knoll Press, New Castle, DE, 1997.

Harding, D. W. 'Regulated Hatred: an Aspect of the Work of Jane Austen', *Scrutiny. A Quarterly Review* 8:4 (1940), 346–62.

Jenkyns, Richard. *A Fine Brush on Ivory: An Appreciation of Jane Austen*. Oxford University Press, 2004.

Johnson, Claudia L. *Equivocal Beings: Politics, Gender and Sentimentality in the 1790s: Wollstonecraft, Radcliffe, Burney, Austen*. University of Chicago Press, 1995.

    Jane Austen. Women, Politics and the Novel. Chicago University Press, 1988.

Kaplan, Deborah. *Jane Austen among Women*. Baltimore: Johns Hopkins Press, 1992.

Kirkham, Margaret. *Jane Austen: Feminism and Fiction.* Sussex: Harvester Press, 1983; repr. London: Athlone Press, 1997.

Knox-Shaw, Peter. *Jane Austen and the Enlightenment.* Cambridge University Press, 2004.

Lascelles, Mary. *Jane Austen and her Art.* Oxford: Clarendon Press, 1939.

Litz, A. Walton. *Jane Austen: A Study of her Artistic Development.* London: Chatto & Windus, 1965.

Looser, Devoney, ed. *Jane Austen and Discourses of Feminism.* Basingstoke: Macmillan, 1995.

Lynch, Deidre, ed. *Janeites: Austen's Disciples and Devotees.* Princeton University Press, 2000.

Miller, D. A. *Jane Austen, or The Secret of Style.* Princeton University Press, 2003.

Mooneyham, Laura G. *Romance, Language and Education in Jane Austen's Novels,* New York: St Martin's Press, 1988.

Mudrick, Marvin. *Jane Austen: Irony as Defense and Discovery.* Princeton University Press, 1952.

Neill, Edward. *The Politics of Jane Austen.* London: Macmillan, 1999.

Park, You-me and Rajeswari Sunder Rajan, eds. *The Postcolonial Jane Austen.* London and New York: Routledge, 2000.

Pinch, Adela. *Strange Fits of Passion. Epistemologies of Emotion. Hume to Austen.* Stanford University Press, 1996.

Poovey, Mary. *The Proper Lady and the Woman Writer: Ideology as Style in the Works of Mary Wollstonecraft, Mary Shelley and Jane Austen.* University of Chicago Press, 1984.

Said, Edward W. 'Jane Austen and Empire' in *Culture and Imperialism.* New York: Knopf, 1993.

Sales, Roger. *Jane Austen and Representations of Regency England.* London: Routledge, 1994.

Selwyn, David. *Jane Austen and Leisure.* London: Hambledon Press, 1999.

Sulloway, Alison G. *Jane Austen and the Province of Womanhood.* Philadelphia: University of Pennsylvania Press, 1989.

Tanner, Tony. *Jane Austen.* Houndmills: Macmillan, 1986.

Todd, Janet. *Sensibility: An Introduction.* London: Methuen, 1986.

Todd, Janet, ed. *Jane Austen in Context,* Cambridge University Press, 2005.

Trilling, Lionel. 'Mansfield Park' in *Jane Austen. A Collection of Critical Essays,* ed. Ian Watt. Englewood Cliffs, NJ: Prentice-Hall, 1966.

Tuite, Clara. *Romantic Austen: Sexual Politics and the Literary Canon.* Cambridge University Press, 2002.

Van Sant, Ann Jessie. *Eighteenth-Century Sensibility and the Novel. The Senses in Social Context.* Cambridge University Press, 1993.

Waldron. Mary. *Jane Austen and the Fiction of her Time.* Cambridge University Press, 1999.

Wiltshire, John. *Jane Austen and the Body: 'The Picture of Health',* Cambridge University Press, 1992.

  Recreating Jane Austen. Cambridge University Press, 2001.

Index